DOCTORAL STUDY AND GETTING PUBLISHED

Surviving and Thriving in Academia provides short, accessible books for navigating the many challenges, responsibilities and opportunities of academic careers. The series is particularly dedicated to supporting the professional journeys of early and mid-career academics and doctoral students, but will present books of use to scholars at all stages in their careers. Books within the series draw on real-life examples from international scholars, offering practical advice and a supportive and encouraging tone throughout.

Series Editor: Marian Mahat, The University of Melbourne, Australia

Published Titles

Achieving Academic Promotion
Edited by Marian Mahat and Jennifer Tatebe

Getting the Most Out of Your Doctorate: The Importance of Supervision, Networking, and Becoming a Global Academic
Edited by Mollie Dollinger

Coaching and Mentoring for Academic Development
By Kay Guccione and Steve Hutchinson

Women Thriving in Academia
Edited by Marian Mahat

Academic Resilience: Personal Stories and Lessons Learnt from the COVID-19 Experience
Edited by Marian Mahat, Joanne Blannin, Caroline Cohrssen, and Elizer Jay de los Reyes

Academic Mobility and International Academics: Challenges and Opportunities
Edited by Jasvir Kaur Nachatar Singh

The Impactful Academic: Building a Research Career That Makes a Difference
Edited by Wade Kelly

Thriving in Academic Leadership
Edited by Sharmila Pixy Ferris and Kathleen Waldron

Supervising Doctoral Candidates
Edited by Chris Rolph

Building Communities in Academia
Edited by Melina Aarnikoivu and Ai Tam Le

Nurturing Wellbeing in Academia: How to Prioritise Your Mental Health
By Poppy Gibson

FORTHCOMING TITLES

Conceptualising the Academic Self: Beyond Traditional Practices
Edited by Victoria I. Ekpo and David Allan

Thriving as a Neurodivergent Academic: Personal and Professional Journeys
Edited by Sarah Timperley, Jessica Riordan, and Matthew Harrison

DOCTORAL STUDY AND GETTING PUBLISHED

Narratives of Early Career Researchers

EDITED BY

RICHARD FAY
The University of Manchester, UK

And

ACHILLEAS KOSTOULAS
University of Thessaly, Greece

United Kingdom – North America – Japan – India
Malaysia – China

Emerald Publishing Limited
Emerald Publishing, Floor 5, Northspring, 21-23 Wellington Street, Leeds LS1 4DL

First edition 2025

Editorial matter and selection © 2025 Richard Fay and Achilleas Kostoulas.
Individual chapters © 2025 The authors.
Published under exclusive licence by Emerald Publishing Limited.

Reprints and permissions service
Contact: www.copyright.com

No part of this book may be reproduced, stored in a retrieval system, transmitted in any form or by any means electronic, mechanical, photocopying, recording or otherwise without either the prior written permission of the publisher or a licence permitting restricted copying issued in the UK by The Copyright Licensing Agency and in the USA by The Copyright Clearance Center. Any opinions expressed in the chapters are those of the authors. Whilst Emerald makes every effort to ensure the quality and accuracy of its content, Emerald makes no representation implied or otherwise, as to the chapters' suitability and application and disclaims any warranties, express or implied, to their use.

British Library Cataloguing in Publication Data
A catalogue record for this book is available from the British Library

ISBN: 978-1-83608-769-4 (Print)
ISBN: 978-1-83608-766-3 (Online)
ISBN: 978-1-83608-768-7 (Epub)

INVESTOR IN PEOPLE

CONTENTS

About the Editors — xi
About the Contributors — xiii

1. Doctoral Study and Getting Published: Narrative and Ecological Perspectives — 1
   Richard Fay and Achilleas Kostoulas

2. Local and Global Challenges for Early Career Publishing — 15
   Jane Andrews

Part A: Finding or Constructing a Researcher Identity

3. The Interacting Selves in Early Career Publishing and Beyond: The Search for a Researcher Identity — 31
   Magdalena De Stefani

4. Where Are You From? — 43
   Eljee Javier

Commentary to Part A — 53
Richard Fay and Achilleas Kostoulas

Part B: The Experience of Writing

5. 'On Being Published': A Reflection on Trajectories of (Published) Texts and Researcher Imaginaries — 57
   Jessica Bradley

6. A Garden of Forking PhD Paths — 69
   Edd Aspbury-Miyanishi

7. Publish, Not Perish: Developing a Purposeful Approach to Doctoral Publications — 77
   Magdalena Rostron

Commentary to Part B — 89
Richard Fay and Achilleas Kostoulas

Part C: Engaging With Co-Authors and Critical Peers

8. Writing and Publishing Collaboratively: A Safe Scaffold for an ECR — 95
   Siti Masrifatul Fitriyah

9. The Benefits of 'Being Shaped' as an Early Career Researcher — 103
   Dylan Williams

10. My Successful and Less Successful Publication Experiences — 113
    Sutraphorn Tantiniranat

Commentary to Part C — 121
Richard Fay and Achilleas Kostoulas

Part D: Building or Joining an Academic Community

11. Developing Researcherhood and Professional Belonging Through Publication — 125
    Zhuo Min Huang

12. Building Your 'LOOP' in Navigating an Academic Community — 137
    Rui He

13. How Practice Shapes Research and a Sense of
    Community in the Field of English for Academic
    Purposes   147
    Paul Breen

Commentary to Part D   155
Richard Fay and Achilleas Kostoulas

Part E: Engaging With Publishers

14. Dilemmas and Challenges in Publication and
    Revision of Research Articles as an Early Career
    Researcher   159
    Duygu Candarli

15. Seeking Constructive Rejections: A Reflection on
    My Publication Strategies During the PhD   169
    Felix Kwihangana

16. It Is Not Easy to Learn About Your Academic Self
    Through the Eyes of Reviewers   179
    Mira Bekar

17. It's Not About Me   191
    Paul Vincent Smith

Commentary to Part E   199
Richard Fay and Achilleas Kostoulas

18. Concluding Comments   203
    Mira Bekar

ABOUT THE EDITORS

Richard Fay is a Reader in Education (TESOL and Intercultural Education) at The University of Manchester (UK), where he received his PhD in Education (2004). He specialises in: language teacher education, intercultural communication/education, researcher education and ethnomusicology. He has coordinated the Lantern research group for the last 20 years.

Achilleas Kostoulas is an applied linguist at the University of Thessaly (Greece). He has published several monographs and edited collections about language education, including *The Intentional Dynamics of TESOL* (2021, De Gruyter; with Juup Stelma) and *Challenging Boundaries in Language Education* (2019, Springer).

ABOUT THE CONTRIBUTORS

Jane Andrews is a Professor of Education at the University of the West of England (UK) and received her PhD in Education (2005) from The University of Manchester (UK). She jointly leads UWE's EdD programme. She specialises in multilingualism and learning including children's experiences of being multilingual and the languaging of research.

Edd Aspbury-Miyanishi, after teaching English for 14 years, returned to university for an MA TESOL followed by a PhD in Education (2023) at The University of Manchester (UK). He is now a Teaching Fellow in TESOL at the University of Leeds (UK). He specialises in the acquisition and development of expertise in teaching.

Mira Bekar is an Associate Professor of Applied Linguistics at Ss. Cyril and Methodius University (R. N. Macedonia) and obtained her PhD (2015) at the Purdue University (USA). She specialises in qualitative research methods, academic L1/L2 writing, online communication and (critical) discourse analysis. She publishes in Macedonian and English.

Jessica Bradley is a Senior Lecturer in Literacies and Language in the School of Education at the University of Sheffield. A linguist by training, her research explores linguistic landscapes in collaboration with creative practitioners, as well as everydayness and belonging through the arts, with a particular interest in multilingualism. Her publications include the co-edited book, *Translanguaging as Transformation: The Collaborative Construction of New Linguistic Realities* (2020, Multilingual Matters).

Paul Breen is a Senior EAP Digital Learning Developer in the Academic Communication Centre at University College, London (UK) and gained his PhD in Education (2014) from The University of Manchester (UK) focusing on EAP, Educational Technology and Teacher Development. He also writes regularly about current affairs and issues relating to Social Justice.

Duygu Candarli is currently a Lecturer in TESOL at the University of Southampton (UK) and gained her PhD in Education from The University of Manchester (UK). She specialises in: second language writing, writing assessment, corpus linguistics and academic discourse. She co-authored *The Linguistic Challenge of the Transition to Secondary School* (2023, Routledge).

Magdalena De Stefani holds a PhD in Education (2012) from The University of Manchester (UK) and is an English teacher and the head of a school in Uruguay. Her research interests include teacher development, action research and narrative approaches, as well as the role of leadership practices in school effectiveness.

Siti Masrifatul Fitriyah is a Senior Lecturer in Education at the Faculty of Education, University of Jember (Indonesia), and obtained her PhD in Education (2017) from The University of Manchester (UK). Her research interests include: language policy and planning, teacher education, bilingual education, narrative inquiry and researching multilingually.

Rui He is a Lecturer in International Education at The University of Manchester (UK) and gained her PhD (2021) from the University of Glasgow (UK). Working as a cross-cultural psychologist, she specialises on international students' acculturation and (im)mobility; mental health and well-being; study abroad programmes; language, culture and identity; and creative research methods.

Zhuo Min Huang is a Senior Lecturer in Intercultural Education at The University of Manchester (UK) where she received her PhD in Education (2019). Her research interests involve: intercultural education, intercultural ethics, epistemic injustice, intercultural mindfulness, intercultural personhood and creative methods.

Eljee Javier is a Senior Lecturer and the Head of English Language at the University of Sussex (UK) and holds an MA in TESOL, an MSc in Educational Research and a PhD in Education (all from The University of Manchester, UK). She specialises in: raciolinguistics, language teacher identities and narrative-based research approaches.

Felix Kwihangana is a Senior Lecturer in Transnational Education at King's College London. He obtained his PhD in Education (2021) and an MA TESOL (Educational Technology), both from The University of Manchester (UK). His research and scholarship focus on teacher education, education policy and digital education in challenging contexts.

Magdalena Rostron is a Visiting Assistant Professor at Georgetown University in Qatar and obtained her PhD in Education (2019) from The University of Manchester (UK). She has interests in: writing and literature; education, culture and politics; exile; and the concept of the Other. She currently researches the impact of architecture on Qatari society.

Paul Vincent Smith is a Lecturer in Education at The University of Manchester (UK) where he gained his PhD in Education (2013). His research interests are in academic writing, higher education policy and practice and theories of learning. He identifies as a sociologist and prefers ethnographic methodologies, as inspired by Garfinkel, Wittgenstein and Dewey.

Sutraphorn Tantiniranat (Khwan) is the English for Communication Graduate Program Chair, Burapha University (Thailand). She received her PhD in Education (2017) from The University of Manchester (UK). Her research focuses on intercultural aspects of the English Language, English as a Lingua Franca (ELF) and appropriate paradigms for teaching English in Thailand.

Dylan Williams is a Lecturer at Queen Mary University of London (UK) and gained his PhD in Education (2020) from The University of Manchester (UK). With a focus on multilingualism and language education, his research uses critical sociological perspectives to explore the interplay between agency and structure of language use in education.

1

DOCTORAL STUDY AND GETTING PUBLISHED: NARRATIVE AND ECOLOGICAL PERSPECTIVES

RICHARD FAY[a] AND ACHILLEAS KOSTOULAS[b]

[a]The University of Manchester, UK
[b]University of Thessaly, Greece

For early career researchers (ECRs) to thrive in academia, the challenge of publishing begins during their doctoral studies. Publishing during and from a doctorate can be seen (Håkansson Lindqvist, 2018) as part of the rite of passage, and as a liminal stage in the researcher's development from doctoral student to ECR. It is a process of academic becoming, one which ECRs face both on their own (perhaps fighting with imposter syndrome) and also with others (perhaps with their mentors and alongside their fellow ECRs). Challenging, often frustrating, but potentially also deeply rewarding, this stage in their academic trajectory brings with it expectations (both their own and those of potential employers for example) and benefits (such as increased employability). It is a process for which many may feel under-prepared, a situation this volume seeks to address by bringing together the experiences and wisdom of 'old hands' from one research network. What were the publishing successes and failures of these ECRs? And the challenges they faced and the rewards gained? And their doubts and insights? What can be learnt from those who have gone before?

This book has a strongly narrative dimension. It curates the stories of a group of ECRs as they, in their own voices, reflect on the experience of trying to be published. There are two main reasons for the book's narrative foregrounding. First, 'the narrative mode of discourse is omnipresent in human affairs' (Nash, 1990, p. xi), and 'we spend our lives immersed in narratives – every day, we swim in a sea of stories and tales that we hear or read or listen to or see ...' (Berger, 1997, p. 1). ECRs are no exception. They swim in a similar sea of stories. Second, narratives are not simply omnipresent – they also have a valuable function for those telling them as well as those listening. We 'give meaning to [our] lives and relationships by storying [our] experience' (White & Epston, 1990, p. 13) since narration is 'an ongoing process of making sense of our experience' (Stephenson, 2000, p. 12). The ECRs whose stories are presented in this volume are making sense of their experiences of publishing. As we engage with their stories, we are immersed in the sea of their meaning-making and are beneficiaries of their storied insights.

RICHARD AND NARRATIVE

Thirty years ago, when I (Richard) became a Lecturer in Education, having a PhD was not required. In fact, I did not gain my doctorate for another 10 years, and my early publications were unconnected to any doctoral aspirations. So, my publishing story is not as closely entwined with doing a doctorate as it has been for the ECRs in this volume. But, as I near the end of my career, and as I have become more involved in supporting ECR colleagues, I am curious about how they survive and thrive in an academic world in which PhDs and publications do so much to frame professional development, job security and career advancement.

My doctoral story does, however, have one important connection to this volume. During fieldwork, I became aware of the explanatory power of narratives as my colleagues made sense of their experiences in the international education project I was researching. This encouraged me to embrace the methodological potential of narration. Although the 'narrative turn' (Goodson & Gill, 2011) was clearly evident in the social sciences when I was completing my thesis (Fay, 2004), narrative methodology was in its infancy in my department. Since then, it has become a major strand in the work of our Lantern network (see below). It made sense to keep this narrative anchor for the publishing experiences of ECRs from this network.

The methodological embrace of the sense-making power of narration and narratives can be traced, in the English-medium literature for sure, to the latter part of the last century (Bruner, 1991, 1996; Clandinin, 2007; Clandinin & Connelly, 1991, 2000; Cortazzi, 1994; Dauite & Lightfoot, 2004; Gergen, 2001; Josselson & Lieblich, 1993; McAdams, 1993; Mishler, 1995; Mitchell, 1981; Nash, 1990; Polkinghorne, 1988; Reissman, 1993; Sarbin, 1986). At its heart lies a realisation of the research value of the seemingly universal habit that humans have of making sense of their experience through the stories they tell others about that experience. Whereas courts seek 'the truth and nothing but the truth' in the testimony of witnesses, 'narrative truth' is highly situated – stories are told:

- at particular moments in time – when they are retold later, details may and almost invariably do change;

- in specific contexts – when told in an interview, work experience details may differ from when told at home;

- for particular people – when told to researchers, details may vary from when told to colleagues; and

- for specific reasons – when told to make someone laugh, details may be different from when sharing something similar which has happened to you.

Nonetheless, there are insights to be valued in storied sense-making in the moment as articulated through narration and captured in the resulting narratives.

The researcher stories presented in this volume are situated in *time* (the authors are ECRs), in *context* (the stories have been written by members of the Lantern researcher network, as stimulated by the opportunity of this volume), in *relationship* (the stories have been commissioned by editors (well) known to the writers, and as written for an imagined readership of researchers seeking support to thrive in academic life) and in *purpose* (the authors seek to share personalised insights from their experience of publishing during and from a doctorate). This situatedness is, we argue, part of their strength – they have plausibility, they speak to other ECRs and they articulate what we might describe as narrative truth.

ACHILLEAS AND ECOLOGICAL THINKING

Many doctoral stories begin with a more or less clearly defined future possible self (Nurius, 1986) as an academic. Mine (Achilleas) is different, in that my PhD (Kostoulas, 2014) was driven more by intellectual curiosity than future career ambitions. While working on my master's dissertation, I took an interest in complex systems theory, which had just made a tenuous foothold in applied linguistics (Larsen-Freeman & Cameron, 2008). There was still much work to be done to 'nativise' complexity thinking into language education, and I enjoyed the challenge, which eventually led to Kostoulas (2014, 2018), a worked example of how to use complexity thinking to describe a language school.

The school I described was one with which I was deeply familiar, and one very closely connected to my professional identity. This meant that as I strived to study its unseen dynamics, I was constantly confronted with how whatever I observed in its activity was entangled with my past actions and my developing identity. This brings up an important point that runs throughout the book: the narratives we tell, and the ways in which we narrate ourselves, all connect – sometimes in unseen ways – to the complex web that connects the context and time in which they are articulated, the relationships within which the narrative act takes place and the purposes that the narrative serves, and the storyteller is hard to extract from the story.

These are the seeds of the ecological perspective that holds this collection together: a perspective that places the individual in the centre of an 'ecology of ideas' (Bateson, 1972/2000) and views meaning-making activity and meaning structures in the ecology as being in constant interplay. Describing this theory briefly is a challenge for which an introductory chapter such as this is not particularly suitable (but see Stelma & Kostoulas, 2021, 2024 for more). When applied to the topic of this book, its starting premise is that all the activity that connects our early selves, as aspiring doctoral students, to our future selves as mature academics is a process of *becoming*. In addition to the acquisition of writing, research, and teaching skills, academic becoming also involves changes in our identities, cognitions, and networks. The academic becoming trajectory takes place within a dense web (or 'ecology') of interconnecting expectations, routinised practices, interactions, resources and more. Different configurations of the diverse elements in an ecology will give rise to specific opportunities for action (or 'affordances'), some arising spontaneously and others being produced by our action. For instance, the availability of funds, a supportive mentor, and institutional pressure to increase research output can come together to produce an affordance for writing an article. In this sense, academic becoming emerges from the environment. But at the same time, the emergent activity reshapes the meaning structures around it. For example, dealing with reviewers and editors becomes easier once one has published several articles. Academic becoming, then, is this reciprocal relationship between meaning structures that generate activity and meaning-generating activity, which preserves our identity as agentic beings.

LANTERN

We can think of academic becoming as being situated in an abstract 'ecology of ideas' (Stelma & Kostoulas, 2021). For many doctoral students and ECRs, this ecology can also take a more concrete form, as they might belong to, identify with and participate in one or more researcher networks, which may have institutional, disciplinary, professional, geographic or other anchors or be more distributed. As academic life ebbs and flows, network membership can be quite fluid, and periods of intense network activity may be followed by quieter ones. And as researchers' doctoral studies progress, their participation may peak and then fall away. Nonetheless, such networks, like supervisory relationships, can be powerful shaping influences on researchers and helping them to thrive, not just survive, in academic life. They may shape their experience of publishing and much else besides.

The researchers in this volume have some connection with one such network. Its name, Lantern – LANguage Teacher Education Researcher Network – is more of an indication of its origins than it is a statement of a tightly delineated research area. In some cases, the contributors' association with Lantern has been substantial and long-lasting, in others briefer and more tangential. Nonetheless, Lantern acts as an anchor for the volume, providing a contextual coherence to an otherwise diverse set of researcher narratives. It has its particularities but, in some ways, it stands for all such networks.

OVERVIEW OF THE VOLUME

This volume consists of 15 narratives, which present diverse aspects of academic writing and publishing and academic professional development. These are organised in five thematically linked parts, as well as theoretical contributions that introduce and conclude the volume. Each narrative begins with a short contextualising section, by the editors. Other than that, we have encouraged and respected the various ways in which authors narrate their experiences, resulting in a polyphonic exploration of early researcherhood. Each section concludes with a brief ecologically-framed commentary, which attempts to tease out commonalities and salient themes in the narratives.

The first substantive contribution in the volume is an overview (by Jane Andrews) of the influences that shape the academic publishing trajectories of ECRs. Her chapter surveys the literature on early career publishing and discusses the pressures to publish and the challenges ECRs face as well as good practices that may support them in their endeavours.

Part A of the book focuses on the process of academic becoming. The two narratives, by Magdalena De Stefani and

Eljee Javier, showcase how academic becoming involves (re-) constructing one's identity. For Magdalena this process involved accepting the entanglement of her professional and academic identities, and building on this hybrid identity as she worked with teachers in her professional setting and published in (and with) the academic community. Eljee's narrative explores the complexities of being a native-speaker of English and also a member of a visible ethnic minority. It alerts us to the fact that academic becoming may involve reconciling conflicting perceived identities.

The narratives that make up Part B bring to the fore diverse ways in which ECRs experience writing for publication. The first narrative, by Jessica Bradley, provides insight into how public and private writing helped her to develop her 'writerly identity'. Next, Edd Aspbury-Miyanishi tells the story of how his PhD by publication organically grew in ways that had little resemblance to his original research plan. Magdalena Rostron concludes this part with advice from her writing and teaching experience. Together, they illustrate how the writing process emerges from shaping influences in the environment.

Part C extends this discussion, by looking into the collaborative aspects of academic publishing. In Siti M. Fitriyah's narrative, we follow the publication of a collaboratively written article and gain insight into team dynamics involving seniority, gender, and 'newcomer' status. The following narrative, by Dylan Williams, tells the story of a series of publications that began before his PhD studies and traces the influences from colleagues that shaped his publication trajectory. In the final narrative of the section, Sutraphorn ('Khwan') Tantiniranat tells the story of how her academic network provided support as she experienced the ups and downs of academic publishing. In doing so, these three narratives provide us with examples of how the processes of writing for publication and academic becoming were shaped by affordances in the authors' academic ecology.

Part D of the book brings together three narratives, by Zhuo Min Huang ('Min'), Rui He and Paul Breen, who share a more socially-oriented perspective on the process of becoming an academic. The three narratives offer insights into the challenges of integrating into academic communities but also into the affordances that these communities provide for professional development. They also illustrate how the process of getting published was not only supported by membership in academic communities but also served as a driver for the process of academic becoming. By broadening our conceptual lens to include the communities of which the authors are part, these narratives offer insights into the reciprocal relationship between academic becoming and academic communities.

In Part E, the focus is on the ECRs' experiences with publishers. In addition to their intrinsic value as practical examples, the narratives by Duygu Candarli, Felix Kwihangana, Mira Bekar and Paul Vincent Smith showcase aspects of how academic becoming manifests itself in interactions with others. Duygu initiates this exploration, by sharing her insights into the decision-making processes that led to publication. Next, Felix presents his strategy of purposively submitting articles to top journals, despite expecting rejection, as a means to obtain useful feedback about his research. Mira uses a Labov-inspired frame to share vignettes of her interactions with critical reviewer feedback and highlights issues of epistemic gatekeeping. Lastly, Paul narrates the publication of an article and the way he engaged with peer-reviewers' making sense of what they read.

The volume concludes with a reflective commentary by Mira Bekar, who synthesises the recurring themes in the collection and relates them to the ecological perspective that runs through the book.

In putting together this volume, we have aspired to synthesise a rich polyphonic tapestry of narratives that illuminate how doctoral students and ECRS navigate the complexities of academic writing and publishing. The diverse perspectives shared across the five thematic parts offer a nuanced understanding of the challenges and opportunities inherent in the process of academic becoming. From the negotiation of professional identities and the intricacies of collaborative efforts to the dynamic interactions with publishers, the narratives collectively underscore the significance of both individual agency and ecological influences in shaping scholarly trajectories. We hope that this collection will not only provide insights into the publishing trajectories of ECRs but also serves as a resource for fostering more supportive and nuanced environment for academic development.

ACKNOWLEDGEMENTS

We, the editors, extend our heartfelt thanks to the contributors of this volume for sharing their stories and insights with us and you, the readers. Our gratitude also goes to the participants of the joint 2021 Lantern and University of Stavanger collaborative ECR workshop on writing during, from and as part of the doctorate; their inspiration and input during the project's early stages were invaluable. We further thank Jing Wang for reviewing the manuscript and offering thoughtful feedback. To all the friends and collaborators who supported this project in various ways, we are deeply grateful. Their contributions have significantly enhanced this book; any remaining shortcomings are solely our responsibility.

REFERENCES

Bateson, G. (2000). *Steps to an ecology of mind: Collected essays in anthropology, psychiatry, evolution, and epistemology.* University of Chicago Press. (Original work published 1972).

Berger, A. A. (1997). *Narratives in popular culture, media, and everyday life*. SAGE.

Bruner, J. S. (1991). The narrative construction of reality. *Critical Inquiry, 18*, 1–21.

Bruner, J. S. (1996). *The narrative construal of reality*. Harvard University Press.

Clandinin, D. J. (Ed.). (2007). *Handbook of narrative inquiry – Mapping a methodology*. SAGE.

Clandinin, D. J., & Connelly, F. M. (1991). Narrative and story in practice and research. In D. Schön (Ed.), *The reflective turn: Case studies in and on educational practice* (pp. 258–283). Teachers College Press.

Clandinin, D. J., & Connelly, F. M. (2000). *Narrative inquiry: Experience and story in qualitative research*. Jossey-Bass (Wiley).

Cortazzi, M. (1994). Narrative analysis – State of the art. *Language Teaching, 27*, 157–170.

Dauite, C., & Lightfoot, C. (2004). *Narrative analysis: Studying the development of individuals in society*. SAGE.

Fay, R. (2004). *Stories of emergent cultures of distance learning and collaboration: Understanding the CELSE-Hellenic Open University project*. PhD Thesis. The University of Manchester.

Gergen, K. J. (2001). Self-narration in social life. In M. Wetherall, S. Taylor, & S. J. Yates (Eds.), *Discourse theory and practice: A reader* (pp. 247–260). SAGE.

Goodson, I. F., & Gill, S. R. (2011). The narrative turn in social research. *Counterpoints*, *386*, 17–38.

Håkansson Lindqvist, M. (2018). Reconstructing the doctoral publishing process. Exploring the liminal space. *Higher Education Research & Development*, *37*(7), 1395–1408. https://doi.org/10.1080/07294360.2018.1483323

Josselson, R., & Lieblich, A. (Eds.). (1993). *The narrative study of lives*. SAGE.

Kostoulas, A. (2014). *A complex systems perspective on English language teaching: A case study of a language school in Greece*. PhD Thesis. The University of Manchester.

Kostoulas, A. (2018). *A language school as a complex system: Complex systems theory in English language teaching*. Peter Lang.

Larsen-Freeman, D., & Cameron, L. (2008). *Complex systems and applied linguistics*. Oxford University Press.

McAdams, D. P. (1993). *The stories we live by: Personal myths and the making of the self*. William Morrow.

Mishler, E. G. (1995). Models of narrative analysis: A typology. *Journal of Narrative and Life History*, *5*, 87–123.

Mitchell, W. J. T. (Ed.). (1981). *On narrative*. Chicago University Press.

Nash, C. (Ed.). (1990). *Narrative in culture: The uses of storytelling in sciences, philosophy, and literature*. Routledge.

Nurius, P. (1986). Possible selves. *American Psychologist*, *41*(9), 954–969.

Polkinghorne, D. E. (1988). *Narrative knowing and the human sciences*. SUNY Press.

Reissman, C. K. (1993). *Narrative analysis*. SAGE.

Sarbin, T. R. (Ed.). (1986). *Narrative psychology: The storied nature of human conduct*. Praeger.

Stelma, J., & Kostoulas, A. (2021). *The intentional dynamics of TESOL*. De Gruyter Mouton.

Stelma, J., & Kostoulas, A. (2024). Revisiting complex dynamic systems theory: Empowering language teachers and teaching. *TESOL Journal*, *15*(3), e790.

Stephenson, S. (2000). Narrative. In G. Browning, A. Halcli, & F. Webster (Eds.), *Understanding contemporary society: Theories of the present* (pp. 112–1250). SAGE.

White, M., & Epston, D. (1990). *Narrative means to therapeutic ends*. Norton.

2

LOCAL AND GLOBAL CHALLENGES FOR EARLY CAREER PUBLISHING

JANE ANDREWS

University of the West of England, UK

Anyone undertaking a review of academic articles, books and chapters about the challenges facing doctoral students and early career researchers in getting published will immediately notice that there are many texts which all point to the urgent and multi-faceted nature of this issue. Håkansson Lindqvist (2018) characterises the processes and practices surrounding doctoral publishing as being both part of a rite of passage in the movement from doctoral student to early career researcher and also as a liminal stage in the researcher's development, whereas in this book, the perspective taken is that the process is one of academic *becoming*.

Many studies, however, document the problematic aspects of this stage. The studies published come from a diversity of geographical areas worldwide and from a wide range of disciplines, indicating that both local and global influences are at play. Studies have been conducted in countries including, but not limited to, Canada, China, Indonesia, Iran, New Zealand,

North Cyprus, Vietnam and the United Kingdom. These studies have been conducted within disciplines such as education, academic writing, computer science, ecology, applied linguistics and sociology. The focus in each study tends to be different (e.g., the impact on doctoral completion), and this fact offers an insight into not only the complexity of this area but also the multiplicity of players who are involved. These range from the doctoral students (as ECRs) themselves to academics in their various roles as doctoral supervisors and journal article reviewers, editors and editorial board members, and those who provide academic and language skills training courses for doctoral students. Attention is frequently given to language matters, specifically, the dominance of English in global publishing and also, researchers' own multilingual skills, the distinctive demands of academic writing in articles as opposed to in a thesis, and writing for different audiences within and outside the academy.

Understanding doctoral publishing means understanding the drivers that sustain the writing process (its 'intentionality'; Stelma & Kostoulas, 2021) as well as the influences, both facilitative and challenging, that shape the process. This complex picture includes:

- What external pressures drive early career researchers to publish and what impact do these pressures have?

- What are the challenges facing early career researchers as they negotiate their multilingual identities within English-dominant literacy practices prevalent in academic publishing?

- What good practices are documented as being supportive of early career researchers in terms of 'publishing pedagogies'?

As Kamler (2008) has noted, with a critical eye, there is no shortage of so-called 'how to' texts with tips and tricks for early career researchers to guide them in achieving their first publication. The review in this chapter seeks to look more deeply into the wider ecology of academic publishing for recent doctoral graduates and, in particular, how it impacts those who are bringing into play their multilingual resources. As such, this selective review of previous studies will serve as a backdrop to the first-hand testimonies provided in the subsequent chapters of this book.

EXTERNAL PRESSURES

Many writers (e.g., Horta & Li, 2023; Indrayadi, 2023; Receveur et al., 2024; Shamsi & Osam, 2022) raise the issue that early career researchers are under pressure to publish, and the urgency of this, for their career progression and reputation, is vividly encapsulated in the commonly-repeated phrase 'publish or perish.' This mantra is seen in operation in different contexts around the world (e.g., in the studies cited above in China, Hong Kong, and Macau; Indonesia; Northern Cyprus and France). In these different contexts, the pressure to publish can be embedded within the regulations surrounding doctoral study and even in Indrayadi's study (2023), as a condition of graduation from a doctoral programme. Shamsi and Osam (2022) also set out how doctoral students are pressured to publish by their institutional regulations, in the context of higher education in Northern Cyprus. In such cases, it appears that institutional pressures to publish and their desire for their academics to publish are being 'sedimented' (Stelma & Kostoulas, 2021) into regulations for doctoral study, with the consequences being felt most acutely by doctoral students.

Further pressure is experienced by doctoral students when the requirement to publish specifies that it must be in English rather than the language in which the student conducted their study and research. Horta and Li (2023) note that this pressure to publish in English may also be self-imposed by the students where they feel that it will give them a competitive advantage when it comes to finding an academic post after graduation.

There are consequences, highlighted by Horta and Li (2023), resulting from the normative pressure to publish during or at the end of doctoral studies, in English. There can be a neglect of dissemination opportunities at a more local level, for example, to stakeholders of the research who could benefit from the scholarship generated in a local context. This point is also made by Shamsi and Osam (2022) in a context where English was the medium of instruction and writing for the thesis. Both studies raise the wider ethical question of who benefits from research and who has access to research findings. Local dissemination would also be more likely to take place in local languages and, as such, would be more easily achieved by researchers conducting their studies in the languages they are most familiar with. As Indrayadi's (2023) study reports, researchers may be drawn away from disseminating their findings locally and in local languages due to the perceived lack of prestige in local journals, which may be unindexed in the global academic publication rankings.

According to Horta and Li (2023), the 'gaze' of the researcher is drawn away from research stakeholders because of the normative pressure to publish in globally recognised journals. As noted above, this can result in the research being less available to those who are most likely to be able to act on research findings and bring about improvements in society.

These pressures felt by early career researchers are described as unethical in a paper by Receveur et al. (2024), who highlight how vulnerable researchers are within a system where profits generated from the publishing industry are extracted without being fed back into it to support those in the early stages of their careers. Receveur et al. (2024) conclude their paper with a proposed portfolio of actions which they offer for both established and early career researchers to adopt in order to bring about system-wide change. The actions operate at the individual level and include: raising awareness of how the system works and what its flaws are and encouraging experienced academics to refuse to publish in journals which have unethical practices or to review for them.

Critiques of the status quo in the publishing world in which early career researchers find themselves include a consideration of the impact of negative practices on the future development of the researcher and on research cultures. Horta and Li (2023) suggest that the development of the researcher's academic identity can be affected by their publishing experience at this early stage. In a similar vein, Huang (2021) reports doctoral researchers prioritising publishing articles above completing their doctoral thesis, due to institutional pressures already discussed. Should these doctoral researchers progress into academic careers? There is the risk that they may encourage and perpetuate the same mentality in their own doctoral students.

The normative pressures in the academic ecology also impact the doctoral students' relationships with both supervisors and fellow doctoral students. In these pressurised contexts, according to Horta and Li (2023), supervisors can be characterised not as supporters of the doctoral researcher as they work on their doctoral thesis but as sources of information regarding publishing. In this context, Horta and Li note that peers can be seen only as rivals in the competitive world of publishing rather than as colleagues who might provide encouragement and support in tackling challenges together.

CHALLENGES

The well-documented dominance of English as the medium for academic publication (e.g., Curry & Lillis, 2017) can present particular challenges for doctoral students and ECRs seeking to publish their research. Hyland (2011) and Hoang and Ma (2019) highlight these challenges as including meeting English language standards required by journals and following the norms of discipline-specific rhetorical structures.

It is important, however, to pause and reflect on the variety of linguistic ecologies doctoral writers are studying in and how/if they are already moving between their different linguistic resources even before they embark on publishing. These contexts tend to be characterised as Anglophone and non-Anglophone at the level of the state, but we also need to consider, at the institutional level, doctoral degree programmes delivered through the medium of English (English Medium Instruction) within countries where English is not an official language.

Research has been conducted in different linguistic contexts for doctoral study and different issues have been identified as presenting challenges for doctoral students engaging in publishing either during or after completion of their studies. On the one hand, Hoang and Ma (2019) document the experiences of Vietnamese doctoral students studying in Australia through the medium of English as they develop strategies to begin publishing their work, also in English. In their research, Hoang and Ma (2019) heard from doctoral writers who felt that they felt more confident about meeting the linguistic challenges of writing for publication than writing in a logical way that would be valued by article reviewers who are the gatekeepers. The implication is that the experience of studying in an Anglophone context has provided a benefit here.

On the other hand, Indrayadi (2023) reports on the experiences of doctoral students in Indonesia completing their studies through the medium of Indonesian. In that study, respondents reported facing challenges in four areas when they attempted to develop a publication in English from their research. These four areas were more wide-ranging in nature than the challenges identified in Hoang and Ma's study and were as follows: (a) title formulation, (b) funding, (c) methodology knowledge, and (d) (English) language.

From these brief examples, we can begin to see how the move into publishing in English language journals may be experienced in quite different terms in different settings. There is an indication here of inequity built into the doctoral publishing experiences of doctoral graduates situated in different academic ecologies.

There are several studies which explore the strategies doctoral researchers from these different contexts use to make the move from writing a thesis to achieving success in academic publishing in English.

The participants in Indrayadi's study (2023) report either using Google Translate to support their academic writing in English or paying a translator to translate their Indonesian language academic writing into English. Both of these strategies can be considered to be problematic. While the former approach may put the integrity of the original work at risk by relying on a tool generated for general-purpose communication rather than academic communication, the latter clearly places a financial burden on the researchers involved. Further financial costs are reported in Indrayadi (2023) where payment to access relevant databases to support the research and evidence base cited in post-doctoral publications is reported as a challenge by the study's participants. It can be seen here that the infrastructure which supports successful academic publishing, such as access to databases, is clearly unequally available to doctoral researchers around the world.

Any assumptions about an advantage experienced by doctoral researchers studying through the medium of English are rapidly dispelled in the study by Shamsi and Osam (2022). Their participants report challenges such as needing to learn the genre of writing an article and becoming aware of how this differs from the expectations associated with writing a thesis. The additional challenge experienced by researchers in different disciplines was also reported, whereby some disciplines offered a wider range of English-language journals in which to publish compared to other disciplines. A final aspect of the challenges reported in Shamsi and Osam (2022) is that while their participants were studying through the medium of English, they had not all completed their prior education, for example, their Master's level study, in English. This meant that while studying for their doctorates, these students were continuing to develop their academic English skills, a process which needs to continue as they move from being a doctoral student into being an early career researcher.

GOOD PRACTICES

Having explored some of the reported challenges experienced by doctoral writers and the self-developed strategies they have employed, we now move on to review what educational practice exists to support doctoral writers in their publishing endeavours. Aitchison, Kamler and Lee (2010) produced a collection of theorised publishing practices under the umbrella term of 'publishing pedagogies'. This term emphasises the broad and growing interest in the area of how doctoral writers learn and develop their skills in gaining publishing success and who the people to support this success might be and what practices are likely to work. A note of caution is offered by Zhang and Curry (2022), however, as they warn that further work is needed to offer robust evaluations of which interventions support doctoral publishing evidence effectiveness.

The interventions reported and the strategies developed by doctoral writers (e.g., Aitchison et al., 2010; Hoang & Ma, 2019; Indrayadi, 2023) include well-known pedagogic practices such as coaching, scaffolding, mentoring and what Wang, Liardét, Lum & Riazi (2024) propose is called 'collaborative co-authorship'. At the heart of these practices lies the aspiration that novice doctoral writers will benefit from the wisdom and guidance of a more experienced other, perhaps the doctoral supervisor or another discipline-specific expert with successful experience in publishing.

There are, of course, assumptions at play here relating to the availability of such experts as resources and the time being allocated for this supportive work with doctoral writers. When doctoral supervisors are themselves subject to accountability pressures about their research performance, referred to by Huang (2021) as a neoliberal publishing habitus, their willingness and availability to support their doctoral and post-doctoral students in publishing is very likely to be variable. Where the resources are available for supervisors to co-author or collaborate on writing with doctoral writers, Kamler (2008) reminds us of the variation across disciplines in terms of how well-respected co-authorship is or not.

An additional approach to supporting doctoral writers is documented as the provision of dedicated spaces or opportunities for the development of the skills required for success in doctoral publishing. Writing groups and writing retreats are examples of such events and Murray (2014) has developed the concept of writing as a social process where development occurs within a safe, supportive group who share their processes with each other in real time. The social writing approach is another example of a publishing pedagogy; however, the emphasis might be seen to be on doctoral writers taking charge of their own development, in cooperation with their peers, which is in contrast to the coaching/mentoring techniques referred to above. A cooperative approach is likely to avoid some of the ethical issues which may arise when the mentor and doctoral writer are in a hierarchical relationship with a power imbalance. A further advantage of a socialising approach to writing in groups may be to have a positive impact on the motivation and well-being of doctoral writers. Indrayadi's study (2023) highlighted a need for writing retreats to reduce doctoral writers' anxiety which hints at a pastoral need alongside the more practical, skills-based needs during this period of a doctoral writer's development.

CONCLUSION

Until the system-wide change called for by Receveur et al. (2024) is carried out, doctoral and post-doctoral researchers are likely to continue to experience both the normative pressure to publish, probably in English, and the challenges of doing so in a competitive environment. As one of Indrayadi's (2023) participants reported, their main obstacle to publishing in international journals was the requirement to accomplish it in English. However, as long as this is the publishing status quo, as Horta and Li warn below, there are consequences for the ethical sharing of knowledge currently and for the future functioning of academia:

> *...[the] culture is endangering global academia, passing on an arguably short-sighted performative ideology to future academics and diverting them from expected and taken-for-granted academic norms of advancing knowledge for the benefit of human welfare. (Horta & Li, 2023, p. 279)*

Indrayadi (2023) concurs with Horta and Li's point that publication locally, and in local languages, is essential for effective dissemination of knowledge and that it is to the detriment of the research itself if it is only disseminated in English. The way to resolve this challenge, for Indrayadi, is to value and respect local publication, in local languages, as a complement to international publication in English, or – in other words – create an ecology with more diverse affordances for publication. Alongside this recommendation, we can reflect on the responsibilities of higher education institutions themselves regarding how doctoral students' achievements are recognised. For Horta and Li (2023), this could involve the implementation of policies which de-prioritise publications as a measure of doctoral success in favour of a broader set of indicators of achievement.

Having set out some of the challenges which doctoral writers may face in a globalised, Anglo-centric academic context, the following chapters provide case studies of how 15 doctoral writers have negotiated their individual paths through this complex terrain.

REFERENCES

Aitchison, C., Kamler, B., & Lee, A. (2010). *Publishing pedagogies for the doctorate and beyond*. Routledge.

Curry, M. J., & Lillis, T. (Eds.). (2017). *Global academic publishing: Policies, perspectives and pedagogies*. Multilingual Matters.

Håkansson Lindqvist, M. (2018). Reconstructing the doctoral publishing process. Exploring the liminal space. *Higher Education Research & Development*, 37(7), 1395–1408. https://doi.org/10.1080/07294360.2018.1483323

Hoang, T. V. Y., & Ma, L. P. F. (2019). Experiences of publishing in English: Vietnamese doctoral students' challenges and strategies. *Across the Disciplines*, 16(3), 50–66. https://doi.org/10.37514/ATD-J.2019.16.3.14

Horta, H., & Li, H. (2023). Nothing but publishing: The overriding goal of PhD students in mainland China, Hong Kong, and Macau. *Studies in Higher Education*, 48(2), 263–282. https://doi.org/10.1080/03075079.2022.2131764

Huang, Y. (2021). Doctoral writing for publication. *Higher Education Research & Development*, 40(4), 753–766. https://doi.org/10.1080/07294360.2020.1789073

Hyland, K. (2011). Welcome to the machine: Thoughts on writing for scholarly publication. *Journal of Second Language Teaching and Research*, 1(1), 58–68.

Indrayadi, T. (2023). Doctoral students' challenges in preparing and publishing research in reputable international journals. *Issues in Educational Research*, 33(3), 1012–1029.

Kamler, B. (2008). Rethinking doctoral publication practices: Writing from and beyond the thesis. *Studies in Higher*

Education, *33*(3), 283–294. https://doi.org/10.1080/03075070802049236

Murray, R. (2014). *Writing in social spaces: A social processes approach to academic writing*. Routledge.

Receveur, A., Bonfanti, J., D'Agata, S., Helmstetter, A. J., Moore, N. A., Oliveira, B. F., Petit-Cailleux, C., Rievrs Borges, E., Schultz, M., Sexton, A. N., & Veytia, D. (2024). David versus Goliath: Early career researchers in an unethical publishing system. *Ecology Letters*, *27*, e14395. https://doi.org/10.1111/ele.14395

Shamsi, A. F., & Osam, U. V. (2022). Challenges and support in article publication: Perspectives of non-native English-speaking doctoral students in a "publish or no degree" context. *Sage Open*, *12*(2). https://doi.org/10.1177/21582440221095021

Stelma, J., & Kostoulas, A. (2021). *The intentional dynamics of TESOL*. De Gruyter.

Wang, J., Liardét, C., Lum, J., & Riazi, M. (2024). Co-authorship between doctoral students and supervisors: Motivations, reservations, and challenges. *Higher Education Research & Development*. https://doi.org/10.1080/07294360.2024.2354253

Zhang, T., & Curry, M. J. (2022). How do we know (if) it works? A review of research evaluating publishing pedagogies for multilingual writers. *Journal of Second Language Writing*, *58*, 100917. https://doi.org/10.1016/j.jslw.2022.100917

Part A

FINDING OR CONSTRUCTING A RESEARCHER IDENTITY

3

THE INTERACTING SELVES IN EARLY CAREER PUBLISHING AND BEYOND: THE SEARCH FOR A RESEARCHER IDENTITY

MAGDALENA DE STEFANI

Ivy Thomas Memorial School, Uruguay

Who am I as a researcher? Who am I as an educator? How do these roles manifest themselves in my published identity? In her story, Magdalena ('Made') asks many questions about her emerging educational–researcher identity. Today, she is a Head Teacher in a Uruguayan school where she previously taught. Her PhD study (De Stefani, 2012) – the first University of Manchester PhD to be undertaken 'in-context' (i.e., by distance learning mode) – fused her teacher education and researcher roles, both of which are underpinned by a desire to promote social justice. After completion, Made remained active in the Lantern community, balancing

(*Continued*)

> (*Continued*)
>
> her academically informed professional identity with her practice-focused researcher identity.
>
> We, the editors, have known Made in various roles over the many years and have witnessed her journey of identity articulation. Richard first met Made before her MA studies and later served as the internal examiner for her viva. Achilleas was an in-context student starting shortly after Made, and they published an article on the emergence of a doctoral student community in a blended learning context (Breen, De Stefani, & Kostoulas, 2011). After her studies, Made continued to publish, individually and with Lantern members. Most recently, with Richard, she has published a chapter (De Stefani, Fay, & Huang, 2024) connected to the social justice themes of her thesis. Being based in her professional context (rather than in the university itself) for her research activities has raised many questions of professional–researcher identity for Made, and her story tells how she engaged with them.

NAVIGATING TOWARDS AN IDENTITY

In the early stages of my doctoral research, I was fortunate to be part of a team of experienced researchers working on topics unfamiliar to me, and I had the chance to publish with fellow students about our 'in-context' doctoral experiences (Breen, De Stefani, & Kostoulas, 2011). These opportunities provided invaluable lessons in research and publishing, shaping my expectations, and highlighting the skills I needed to develop.

The publishing process initially seemed overwhelming, and I was grateful for the guidance of colleagues who were more experienced and efficient in managing the details and systematicity of academic work. Publishing with more experienced colleagues, I particularly enjoyed the teamwork, learning about myself in the process. I discovered that while I was not particularly good at handling details, I was quite adept at integrating different bits of information. I deeply admired my fellow students who were so much more systematic than me, and I came to value how our joint efforts made us complementary. As a doctoral student, I was exposed to a myriad of research projects and approaches, gradually discovering my primary interests. I was often inspired by the researchers and methodologies I encountered, experiencing what Channa (2017, p. 365) describes as 'shifting ideological and epistemological orientations toward research due to the readings and discussion of the course.'

After completing my thesis and obtaining my doctorate, I felt there was an expectation to publish my research. However, my interest in the original topic had waned, and the thesis writing process had left me exhausted. Even though the doctorate had gone very smoothly, the final stages were not easy. I felt unsure about my preparedness for the viva, which may have made me perceive it as a difficult and stressful experience – one that, in hindsight, did not fully reflect the overall process. Looking back now, I can appreciate and remember my PhD journey quite fondly. However, when I tried to go back to my research to continue exploring the topic, it was difficult for me to find any motivation in it. Notably, only one of my journal publications is related to my doctoral research (Armellini & De Stefani, 2016).

I also explored collaborative opportunities with other researchers at a regional level, taking part in diverse projects, such as the creation of an action research network in Latin America (Banegas, De Stefani, Troncoso, Rebolledo, & Smith, 2020; De Stefani, 2020), which felt promising and aligned well with my area of expertise. Another promising collaboration involved two renowned senior researchers (Aguerrondo, Vaillant, De Stefani, & Azpiroz, 2014), but this experience highlighted the contrast between my role as a student in an international university and the more established researchers' approaches in the region. Throughout, I was partly driven by my need to find a specific area of interest, thinking it was important to shape a predictable research path and become a 'specialist' in an area within education. However, these and other experiences helped me to understand that exploring different educational issues through various collaborations provided valuable learning opportunities and a broader perspective on educational research. While I initially viewed this non-specialist approach as less prestigious, it broadened my understanding and contributed to my growth as a researcher.

Over time, my professional role expanded to include educational leadership. As this happened, my career as an educational manager became increasingly captivating, and I felt a natural inclination to conduct research on my experiences working with teachers in a school setting. Yet, having a primarily executive rather than academic role made it challenging to find the time and resources to conduct research despite the occasional publications I managed to produce (e.g., De Stefani, 2014). Whenever opportunities arose to work within a team, I welcomed them, even if the topics were not as interesting as my 'real life' school context. These collaborative experiences helped to shape and expand my perspective on educational research.

TELLING THE STORIES OF OUR THEORISATIONS: INSIGHTS FROM ACTION AND NARRATIVE RESEARCH

After completing my doctorate, action research and action learning became central to my approach, aligning with the practical demands of my work environment, where application was key (McNiff, 2013; Pedler, Burgoyne, & Brook, 2005; Revans, 1982; Zuber-Skerritt, 2002). Theorising through action, striving for the common good, and collaborating with others were vital in my quest to establish my identity as a researcher. I successfully found my voice as an action researcher within my work context, which was personally fulfiling. However, balancing the responsibilities of running a school full-time with the demands of a young family made it increasingly difficult to devote time to publishing. At this point, my academic pursuits received little support from my job description, colleagues, or institution, which led to growing frustration.

My interest in narrative research was initially sparked during my PhD when I learnt about my fellow students' work, particularly a colleague's study on the life stories of Yemeni women (Halldórsdóttir, 2014). It was not long before I felt compelled to experiment with narrative in the accounts of my action research journeys, which can be seen in my endeavour to narrate the joint action research process with a colleague at the school where I work (De Stefani, 2014). However, it was through the Lantern community that I was introduced to narrative research as a means of understanding experiences in various educational contexts (e.g., Palacios, Onat-Stelma, & Fay, 2021), and I was invited to collaborate on a project that recently led us to combine narrative perspectives with arts-based research to explore the identities of teacher-artists in my home country (De Stefani, Fay, & Huang, 2024).

Over the years, and while taking part in various individual and collaborative projects, at times I felt the tension between the action researcher and the narrative researcher. Rather than viewing these as dichotomous, however, I adopted an integrated perspective, recognising that both action and narrative approaches continuously shape my identity as an educator. I value the power of action and reflection in creating a virtuous circle that leads to theorisation. Similarly, I find narratives immensely powerful, as the stories we tell and how we tell them shape our thinking and influence our professional identities, allowing for 'accessibility, transferability, and critical analysis' (Franks, 2016, p. 1). Consequently, I believe that the interplay between action and narrative research has also contributed to my unique researcher identity.

SHIFTING PERSPECTIVES: EMBRACING AN ECLECTIC RESEARCHER IDENTITY

Twelve years after obtaining my doctoral degree, I find myself navigating a diverse research journey that defies conventional paths I once considered the 'right' way. My experience spans eclectic research interests, influenced by my managerial role rather than an academic position, which has somewhat constrained extensive publishing. Nevertheless, upon reflection, I recognise how my roles as both a researcher and educational manager continually enrich each other, fostering a dynamic interplay that shapes my professional trajectory.

Embracing this journey has meant accepting my identity as a researcher with an eclectic profile. Through introspection, I have come to value my diverse expertise as an asset rather than a limitation. I take pride in engaging in a variety of research projects, drawing strength from teamwork, which has been integral to my identity formation and has yielded both personal and professional growth. Collaborating with colleagues from diverse backgrounds has enhanced my intercultural understanding and communication skills, as well as my ability to navigate nuanced professional relationships (Christie et al., 2007, p. 266). As a participant in a community of practice (Lave & Wenger, 1991; Wenger, 1998), I have cultivated shared understandings and gained a sense of agency, crucial for balancing the demands of my job, family, and research aspirations.

Currently, I am focused on integrating and applying lessons learnt throughout my research career, refraining from self-judgement and remaining reflexive about my evolving researcher profile. I actively seek collaborative opportunities while continuing to explore potential areas of expertise that resonate with my evolving interests. Yet, my most significant growth stems from embracing the unique aspects of my professional reality and recognising them as strengths.

PRESTIGE VS LEARNING: WHAT I WISH I HAD KNOWN AS AN EARLY CAREER ACADEMIC

In the above narrative, I explored how my researcher identity and publishing endeavours have been shaped since the early years of my career. I can deconstruct my experience by describing the three 'selves' that influenced my decisions: the doctoral student, the emerging researcher and the educational leader.

- My *doctoral student self* was a defining force throughout the early days of my profession. While focusing on my own doctoral study constrained my experience to some extent, I continued to search for my voice and broadened my horizons by learning about other students' experiences and explorations.

- My *emerging researcher identity*, coupled with the self-imposed expectation to find a research passion, also influenced my thinking and decisions after my doctorate. I welcomed opportunities to collaborate with others, even if the research area was not of particular interest or close to my expertise. This led me to engage in enriching projects with colleagues but also diverted me from my intention to find a specific area of interest.

- Finally, *my educational leader self*, or 'the real-life me', grew increasingly important over time. I embraced my instinct to listen to teachers' voices as I tried to find my own, seeking opportunities to publish from an action research perspective at first and gradually turning my attention towards narrative research.

I conclude by reflecting on how I have made sense of this journey, in the hope that it will encourage ECRs to reflect on their own identity formation by constructively examining their choices and experiences.

We live in a world where transparency, information and data have become absolute priorities. From evidence-based research to transparency in architecture, the ubiquity, excess and immediacy of information have become a way of life (Han, 2015). More than ever, publishing is needed as evidence to demonstrate a researcher's existence and value, as has been extensively discussed in the recent publish or perish literature (e.g., Aprile, Ellem, & Lole, 2021; Bello, Azubuike, & Akande, 2023; Van Dalen & Henkens, 2012). This endless competition for researchers to be 'seen' through publications is very much in line with today's society, where social media has taught us that if something is not visible, it can barely claim its own existence (Han, 2015). The impact of this view has been so negative on academia that some authors maintain publishing needs to restore its real purpose so that it can make 'lasting contributions to the betterment of society' (Elbanna & Child, 2023, p. 614) and not only serve as some kind of display window.

For early career researchers navigating the pressures of a 'publish or perish' culture, I acknowledge the formidable challenges and stress involved. However, I advocate for a constructive approach that values diverse research paths and encourages reflection on one's professional journey. I wish I had known earlier on that a relentless pursuit of novelty and high-impact publications can sometimes overshadow the intrinsic joy of discovery and the value of deep learning. Through experience, I have found that achieving a balance between our own expectations of academic prestige and our genuine intellectual curiosity enhances personal fulfilment. Moreover, I have come to appreciate how collaboration and team diversity foster cross-cultural learning and a genuine interest in exploring issues that contribute to the betterment of our society. In academia, success should not be solely measured by publication metrics, but also by our capacity to engage deeply with opportunities that resonate with a broader vision of scholarly development. In this perspective, prioritising personal and collective learning over mere prestige becomes central to our scholarly journeys.

REFERENCES

Aguerrondo, I., Vaillant, D., with De Stefani, M., & Azpiroz, M. (2014). *Aprendizaje efectivo para todos. ¿Cómo lograrlo? Resumen de informe de investigación*. Universidad ORT–Uruguay.

Aprile, K. T., Ellem, P., & Lole, L. (2021). Publish, perish, or pursue? Early career academics' perspectives on demands for research productivity in regional universities. *Higher Education Research & Development*, *40*(6), 1131–1145.

Armellini, A., & De Stefani, M. (2016). Social presence in the 21st century: An adjustment to the Community of Inquiry framework. *British Journal of Educational Technology*, *47*(6), 1202–1216.

Banegas, D., De Stefani, M., Troncoso, C., Rebolledo, P., & Smith, R. (Eds.). (2020). *Horizontes 1: ELT teacher research in Latin America*. IATEFL & British Council. http://resig.weebly.com/uploads/2/6/3/6/26368747/horizontes_ebook.pdf

Bello, S. A., Azubuike, F. C., & Akande, O. A. (2023). Reputation disparity in teaching and research productivity and rewards in the context of consequences of institutionalization of Publish or Perish culture in academia. *Higher Education Quarterly*, *77*(3), 574–584.

Breen, P., De Stefani, M., & Kostoulas, A. (2011). Navigating a pathway to partnership through turbulent seas of adversity. In P. Tripathi & S. Mukerji (Eds.), *Cases on innovations in educational marketing: Transnational and technological strategies* (pp. 273–294). IGI Global.

Channa, L. A. (2017). Letter writing as a reflective practice: Understanding the shuffling, shifting, and shaping of a researcher identity. *Reflective Practice*, *18*(3), 358–368.

Christie, D., Cassidy, C., Skinner, D., Coutts, N., Sinclair, C., Rimpilainen, S., & Wilson, A. (2007). Building collaborative communities of enquiry in educational research. *Educational Research and Evaluation*, *13*(3), 263–278.

De Stefani, M. (2012). *Exploring the possible: Empowering English language teachers in provincial Uruguay through blended learning.* PhD Thesis. The University of Manchester.

De Stefani, M. (2014). Challenging traditions: Constructing an identity through innovative teaching practices. In P. Breen (Ed.), *Cases on teacher identity, diversity, and cognition in higher education* (pp. 258–286). IGI Global.

De Stefani, M. (2020). Leadership and language teacher development. In S. Welsh & S. Mann (Eds.), *The Routledge handbook of English language teacher education* (pp. 596–610). Routledge.

De Stefani, M., Fay, R., & Huang, Z. (2024). English for research purposes and linguistic diversity: Researcher reflexivity and social justice. In P. Breen & M. le Roux (Eds.), *Social justice in EAP and ELT contexts: Global higher education perspectives* (pp. 197–210). Bloomsbury.

Elbanna, S., & Child, J. (2023). From 'publish or perish' to 'publish for purpose'. *European Management Review*, *20*(4), 614–618.

Franks, T. M. (2016). Purpose, practice, and (discovery) process: When self-reflection is the method. *Qualitative Inquiry*, *22*(1), 47–50.

Halldórsdóttir, T. M. (2014). *Stories of our sister selves: How educated Yemeni women experience the storylines available to them.* PhD Thesis. The University of Manchester.

Han, B. C. (2015). *The transparency society.* Stanford University Press.

Lave, J., & Wenger, E. (1991). *Situated learning: Legitimate peripheral participation.* Cambridge University Press.

McNiff, J. (2013). *Action research: Principles and practice.* Routledge.

Palacios, N., Onat-Stelma, Z., & Fay, R. (2021). Extending the conceptualisation of reflection: Making meaning from experience over time. *Reflective Practice, 22*(5), 600–613. https://doi.org/10.1080/14623943.2021.1938995

Pedler, M., Burgoyne, J., & Brook, C. (2005). What has action learning learned to become?. *Action Learning: Research and Practice, 2*(1), 49–68. https://doi.org/10.1080/14767330500041251

Revans, R. W. (1982). *The origins and growth of action learning.* Cherwell Bratt.

Van Dalen, H. P., & Henkens, K. (2012). Intended and unintended consequences of a publish-or-perish culture: A worldwide survey. *Journal of the American Society for Information Science and Technology, 63*(7), 1282–1293.

Wenger, E. (1998). Communities of practice: Learning as a social system. *Systems Thinker, 9*(5), 2–3.

Zuber-Skerritt, O. (2002). The concept of action learning. *The Learning Organization, 9*(3), 114–124.

4

WHERE ARE YOU FROM?

ELJEE JAVIER

University of Sussex, UK

> In the preceding narrative, Magdalena De Stefani outlined her struggle to find a balance between her educational (teacher educator) role and her researcher activities. Eljee's story also poses questions of ECR and (university) teacher identities. In her online Lantern profile, she tells of her experience of applying for overseas teacher (English as a foreign language) posts. As a Filipino-heritage Canadian with English as her first language, she became stuck in a frustrating cycle of 'filling in applications, then gaining acceptance with a request for a photo, sending my photo, and then being rejected.' Finally, one hiring agency explained that 'We don't really hire Asian looking teachers. Sorry'. Her reflexive exploration of this issue began during her MA studies and continued through her doctoral studies (Javier, 2015), which explored the personal and professional identity issues experienced by her and other
>
> (*Continued*)

> (*Continued*)
>
> similarly colleagues, i.e., visibly ethnic minority native English-speaking teachers (VEMNESTs). In her post-doctoral role as a teaching-focused Senior Lecturer in a UK university, how could her research be of most value? Eljee's research focus is one driven by experienced injustice; her subsequent professional focus is one of research impact through teaching. Her journey from doctoral student to early career academic has involved her overcoming a sense of being 'a second-class academic', learning to embrace the value as a research-through-teaching by expanding her sense of 'worth beyond [her] publication outputs.'

MY RESEARCH JOURNEY

My research interests stem from a critical encounter early in my career, where my applications for English language teacher posts outside of Canada were turned down because of my ethnicity as a Filipino-Canadian. Despite English being my first language, my ethnic appearance did not align with the underlying assumption that native English speakers from Canada are white. This assumption made it challenging to find schools in Asia willing to hire me as an English language teacher. These experiences drove me to explore the relationship between race and language and to find out whether others had similar experiences. My doctoral research focused on interrogating the racial assumptions associated with native-English-speaking teachers (e.g., Canadian, American and British), what factors influenced the normalisation of racialised identities related to nationality, 'native English speaker,' and the embedded hierarchies inherent within these terms. More specifically, I wanted to explore how VEMNESTs navigated their professional identities in a field where their legitimacy is often questioned.

DEFINING VEMNEST

I first coined the term VEMNEST in 2007 in an assignment during my postgraduate studies at The University of Manchester. A VEMNEST, by definition, embodies a complex intersection of racial and linguistic identities. The visible aspect refers to the ethnic minority status, making it an external characteristic (e.g., skin colour) easily perceived by others. The native English-speaking part of the term, however, is not always immediately apparent and often requires explanation or justification, especially in contexts (e.g., Canada) where being a native speaker is not typically associated (e.g., by employers) with being a visible ethnic minority. Despite the term VEMNEST being cumbersome, through it I was able to articulate aspects of my identity that I was struggling to unite – who I was a person and what might this mean for me as a professional. It also opened up a path for me to further study and the exploration of the identities of other people 'like me.'

WRITING FOR AND BEYOND THE THESIS

There comes a point in the doctoral thesis writing process where candidates need to actually finish the thesis and stop. With a final submission date looming, I needed to determine what was essential for the thesis and what could be included in 'the book' (i.e., subsequent publications). As I finalised my study, it was difficult decide when 'enough is enough,' knowing that there was still more to learn and doubting whether my work covered everything I wanted. I had to accept that my thesis was actually the start, and not the end, of my research journey. There would be other opportunities to cover 'everything else.' And for me, those opportunities came in the form of publications and teaching opportunities.

My first publication – a short book chapter (Javier, 2010) based on my Master's dissertation – was actually written at the beginning of my PhD. In it, I discussed the idea of the 'foreign-ness' of VEMNESTs and the associations between appearing 'foreign' and 'native speaker' identities. I presented my narrative of working as a Filipino-Canadian ELT in China and the challenges I faced during my employment, which stemmed from looking too 'local.' I didn't look 'foreign': I noted that '... a native speaker is assumed to be a foreigner to the host country and, by assumption, would not look Chinese' (p. 117). This was the first time I had written for an audience unfamiliar with my work, and I faced the challenge of clearly presenting concepts without diminishing their complexity. Fortunately, the editors of the book were supportive during my writing process and asked useful questions to help me consider how to write for the audience rather than for myself. This experience was also invaluable in the final stages of writing my thesis. Keeping in mind that the readers were thesis examiners made it easier (to some extent) to see the main purpose of my thesis and its potential for future research beyond the PhD.

The next book chapter I published (Javier, 2016) was written around the same time as the final draft of my thesis. However, this chapter focused specifically on exploring the assumed racial hierarchies of NESTs and argued that VEMNESTs were 'almost NESTs.' In this chapter, I presented some of the narrative data from my thesis, which enabled me to offer a more nuanced discussion on how these labels are not clear-cut:

> *The stories shared by Andrés and Li (as well as my own story) are examples that demonstrate how we have been accepted as a different 'type' of NEST – one that conforms to the linguistic expectations yet challenges the racial and ethnic identity stereotypes. What is not clear is whether we were attributed equal status to White NESTs or regarded as exceptions. Our experiences reveal a range of different categories of professional identities that exist within the NS/ NNS binary distinction that ought to be acknowledged. (Javier, 2016, p. 237)*

ACADEMIC IDENTITIES: WHO'S WORTH MORE?

Despite the challenges facing UK higher education, I eventually found employment at a UK university. For a number of practical reasons, I have maintained a teaching focus in my career and, consequently, have had fewer opportunities to publish my own research since graduation. As I took on this teaching-focused role, I began to believe I was a second-class academic: those that can't do (i.e., research), teach instead. This belief was at odds with my conviction that the act of teaching is vital to being an educator. This conflict forced me to reckon with my views, and in doing so, I eventually changed how I valued myself as an academic by expanding my worth beyond my publication outputs. In other words, I have come to accept for myself that teaching is as important as research, and that I have been able to continue my research through teaching.

To this end, I have been able to introduce and explore raciolinguistics (Alim, Rickford & Ball, 2016) with my students over the years. For some of them, broaching race-related topics is seen as highly contentious, and through teaching, I have found approaches to create spaces for students to explore sensitive topics. I use my identity research as an example of acknowledging the lived experiences of racialised people. In doing so, students become aware that while discussions of race can be on an abstract level, they cannot be divorced from the reality of being.

POSITIONALITY AND PEDAGOGY

One of the key challenges I faced whilst doing my doctorate was the lack of existing literature on VEMNESTs. My literature review revealed a significant gap in research focusing specifically on the intersection of race and native English-speaking status in Teaching English to Speakers of Other Languages (TESOL). Consequently, I had to draw on broader theories and studies from critical race theory and language identity research. Using narrative-based research methods, I discovered that many VEMNESTs share similar experiences of marginalisation and discrimination. These teachers often contend with prejudiced assumptions that undermine their professional expertise and linguistic abilities. The findings highlighted how deeply ingrained racial biases are in perceptions (within TESOL) of language proficiency and teaching competence.

POSITIONALITY AND TEACHING

Accounting for positionality in what and how we teach is as important as accounting for it in our research. Who I am in the classroom (i.e., who is doing the teaching and learning) – the 'normative assumptions' related to my being a university lecturer, a woman, Filipino, Asian, Canadian (etc.) – is part of what is being taught and learnt. This ecology is an example of the interrelatedness of identities and how intentionality operates. The insights and awareness I've gained from my research have informed how I approach the topics I cover in my classes for the students who join me in learning about racialised identities (as an example). In other words, as a visible ethnic minority (e.g., a 'non-white/non-Caucasian') lecturer, I've been more comfortable exploring topics about race with my students than other colleagues. Perhaps it is because I am a VEM, perhaps it's because I've spent years researching this area or perhaps my lived experience as a VEM has given me more opportunities to discuss race outside the classroom.

Critical reflection has been central to my teaching philosophy. Introducing raciolinguistics to my students has been a vital part of this process. By being open about who I am and my struggles with understanding the terms ascribed to me, I've been able to create a safer space for students to explore race and, in turn, explore their own identities. This approach has been instrumental in fostering a more inclusive and reflective learning environment.

The emergence of raciolinguistics (e.g., Alim, Rickford & Ball, 2016) as a distinct area within applied linguistics has influenced my approach to academic writing. I have found this area to be my academic 'home' in that the intersections between language, race and identity have a name. By engaging with this growing body of scholarship, I am becoming more open and aware to more nuanced and critical arguments from diverse theoretical frameworks and perspectives. Furthermore, I have found the increasing contributions from scholars in the Global South and the study of diverse English to be especially important, as they push me to integrate more global perspectives in my research. While I acknowledge that equity in this field remains an ongoing challenge, my own experience of working with concepts such as VEMNEST has made it easier to access relevant literature and develop more globally informed and reflective scholarship. This growing body of work has helped me frame my academic writing in ways that are more critical of sociopolitical dynamics, encouraging me to question assumptions that may otherwise go unchallenged.

As research into language identities continues to grow, I believe it is crucial for academic writing, including my own, to address the persistent complexities surrounding racial and ethnic identities in English language teaching. In my future work, I am further exploring how the intersections of race, language, and identity play out in different cultural and educational contexts. The impact of global migration and the increasing diversity of English speakers as vital areas for exploration and I have particular interest in understanding how the diverse identities of English language teachers influence their professional practices and interactions with students, as this will enable me to contribute to the development of more comprehensive and inclusive research in applied linguistics.

In summary, my journey as a VEMNEST has been one of personal and professional growth, navigating the complexities of identity in the field of English language teaching. My experiences have underscored the importance of teaching and research in addressing race and language issues. Through both activities, I have sought to create a more inclusive and reflective learning environment for my students and contribute to the growing field of raciolinguistics. As research into language identities continues to expand, I plan to further explore the intersections of race, language and identity and contribute a more nuanced understanding of these dynamics in English language teaching.

REFERENCES

Alim, H. S., Rickford, J. R., & Ball, A. F. (Eds.). (2016). *Raciolinguistics: How language shapes our ideas about race*. Oxford University Press.

Javier, E. (2010). The foreign-ness of native speaking teachers of colour. In D. Nunan & J. Choi (Eds.), *Language and culture: Reflective narratives and the emergence of identity* (pp. 97–102). Routledge.

Javier, E. (2015). *Narratively performed role identities of visible ethnic minority, native English speaking teachers in TESOL*. PhD Thesis. The University of Manchester.

Javier, E. (2016). "Almost" native speakers: The experiences of visible ethnic-minority native English-speaking teachers. In F. Copland, S. Garton, & S. Mann (Eds.), *LETs and NESTs: Voices, views and vignettes* (pp. 227–239). British Council.

COMMENTARY TO PART A

RICHARD FAY[a] AND ACHILLEAS KOSTOULAS[b]

[a]The University of Manchester, UK
[b]University of Thessaly, Greece

For many ECRs, writing for publication is not just an added imposition to the requirements of their doctoral studies, but it is also a process of developing their academic identity. In the two narratives that make up Part A, Magdalena ('Made') De Stefani and Eljee Javier tell the story of their academic *becoming*, that is, of how their academic identities emerged from the expectations, experiences and interactions associated with their writing and publishing endeavours.

Viewed from an ecological standpoint, academic becoming is a process of moving from the state of interacting with academic setting as a student towards the state of interacting as a full member of the community. This is not to say that the endpoint of the process is to assume a uniform, statically defined academic identity – if anything, these two narratives draw our attention to how diverse such identities can be. Rather, the criterion seems to be acceptance (by the person and by the community) of the role in which the individual feels most comfortable in the ecology: for Made, that of a researcher–professional, whose activity creatively subverts the traditional division of labour between school and the academe (Borg, 2010); in Eljee's case, that of a research-informed but teaching-oriented scholar with a focus on challenging racial inequality in TESOL. Such hybrid identities, which defy the stereotype of an academic with a singular drive to research and publish, are increasingly visible despite the neoliberal pressure for bibliographically measurable accountability.

Both narratives express sentiments of unease about the normative pressures to develop a certain publication profile: 'I felt there was an expectation to publish my research' (Made); and 'I began to believe I was a second-class academic' (Eljee). Such sentiments are indicative of how accountability pressures and perceptions of research are ideologically naturalised, as the 'proper' or indeed the only way of being an academic, leading to the 'structuration' (Giddens, 1984) of the neoliberal university. But equally, by showing how an ECR can construct and occupy spaces of *their choosing* in the academic ecosystem, the two narratives offer an example of an alternative, less deterministic way to perceive structure and agency in academic becoming.

REFERENCES

Borg, S. (2010). Language teacher research engagement. *Language Teaching*, 43(4), 391–429.

Giddens, A. (1984). *The constitution of society*. University of California Press.

Part B

THE EXPERIENCE OF WRITING

5

'ON BEING PUBLISHED': A REFLECTION ON TRAJECTORIES OF (PUBLISHED) TEXTS AND RESEARCHER IMAGINARIES

JESSICA BRADLEY

University of Sheffield, UK

> As with many researcher networks, Lantern membership boundaries are fluid. Many of its members do have close affiliations with one university (i.e., Manchester), but several of the storytellers in this volume, Jess being a case in point, form part of an expanding circle, introduced to us through a snowball effect as (former) doctoral students at Manchester develop networks of their own. Her many, typically collaborative, publications include an edited book, a dozen or more journal articles, and some 10 chapters. Some predate her doctoral thesis (e.g., Bradley, 2018), but many have appeared as her post-doctoral career flourished. Her story below does focus on particular published works, but, at its heart, lies a reflection on the imagined character of 'being published'.

In this chapter, I consider writing and publishing, and differing hierarchies of published text, as imagined and reimagined over the course of a doctoral research project. In particular, I explore how the status of 'being published' is imagined. I describe the broader context around a published piece of writing on which I reflect (Bradley, 2015a) and follow with excerpts from my research blog from 2015 (Bradley, 2015b, 2015c) to illustrate how different forms and genres of writing lead to a reflexive and fluid appreciation of the complexity of academic *writerly* identities.

But first, what do I mean by 'imagined'? The idea of an 'imagined community' was conceptualised by Benedict Anderson (1983) to critically describe nationalism and nationalist movements, as well as the highly complex processes involved in creating these communities. Communities, as Anderson states, 'can be distinguished, not by their falsity/genuineness, but by the style in which they are imagined' (p. 6). Whilst nation states are not the focus of this chapter, I do find this to be a useful concept for thinking about how much an academic career, as 'desired' trajectory, relies on both an imagined 'destination' and an imagined community. In this sense multiple 'imaginaries' entangle, as a doctoral researcher or early career researcher, attempts to make sense of what *might* be, what *can* be and *how* one might arrive at this imagined state of being and doing.

WRITING IN A PANDEMIC

At the time the editors asked me to contribute to this edited collection, I was fortunate enough to be at the University of Jyväskylä in central Finland as a visiting researcher, a visit that was made possible through a researcher mobility scheme. It was October 2021 and an unsettling time after the COVID-19 pandemic had disrupted so much that had seemed quite normal and unremarkable, with travel being one of these normal and unremarkable things. I was one of the first scholars to travel to Jyväskylä through the scheme post-pandemic and to 'return' to the kind of transnational mobility that we had very much taken for granted.

At that time masks, social distancing and COVID-19 passports were required for travel, and when I arrived in Helsinki, I found that some restaurants required another kind of passport to allow entry, one that was only possible for EU citizens. During my two-week stay in Jyväskylä, I was welcomed by colleagues with whom I worked to develop ideas, discuss theories, and plan publications. The difference at that moment, as compared with pre-pandemic and now (I write this now in the summer of 2024), was noticeable in the physical distances we kept, the mask dispensers in the entrances to buildings, the COVID-19 signage to which we had so quickly become accustomed in 2020 and the general quietness around the campus and the city. The imagined academic community significantly shifted and changed shape during and after the pandemic, not solely in the experience of academic environments but also with desired identities and these imagined states of being and doing associated with 'being scholarly'.

These circumstances and being 'away' led to some reflection on my part. At the height of the pandemic, I was co-director of an undergraduate programme, teaching, researching, writing and also homeschooling my two children during periods of school building closures. As for so many people, it had been a time of intensity and anxiety, one which my colleague Yinka Olusoga and I have described in a recent book chapter as 'living at work' (2025; see also Olusoga & Bannister, 2023). So being away, being out of the United Kingdom, being alone, and the quieter, subdued, context of travelling at that moment enabled me to think about the work I had done, the work I was doing and the work I wanted to do. I found myself returning to a private blog I had kept as a doctoral researcher a few years before.

BETWEEN PUBLIC AND PRIVATE WRITING

In the 2024 world of Substack newsletters, podcasting, microblogging on Instagram and video sharing through TikTok, the idea of writing on a blog seems somewhat antiquated. At the time I was doing my PhD, however (2014–2018), blogging was perhaps at its height of popularity. Alongside using 'Twitter' (now 'X'), in the mid-2010s academics were encouraged to write online, personally and informally, as a way to explore public engagement and as part of a general movement towards public intellectualism. This crafting and carving of academic thinking online (see Allsop, Rzyankina, Zhao, & Rowsell, 2022, for a discussion of pandemic 'shelfies' and academic online 'performances') also inevitably entailed the blurring and entangling of professional and personal lives and identities.

Prior to starting my doctorate, I had worked for a decade in the more 'public facing' side of academia. In my professional role as an education engagement officer at a Russell Group institution in the north of England I had worked to translate academic research and student education into schools-facing activity, for example supporting academic colleagues to turn their research findings or undergraduate teaching into workshops for young people as part of the University's outreach and widening participation programme.

A blog, therefore, seemed a natural space in which I might document my developing ideas, explore the knotty problems arising through my reading, and grapple with the general chaos and uncertainty of the early stages of doctoral research. Writing 'publicly,' as if in conversation, seemed more natural to me as someone who was used to communicating beyond academia.

At this time, I was also editing the project blog for the research project to which my PhD was linked, but my personal research blog was a private document of my research processes. I started with an open blog (that was visible to anyone who found it), which I also used for more public writing, including writing up research seminars and conferences I had attended or organised. Gradually, I started to make certain blog posts private through adding a password. I did this for a number of different reasons, including concerns around the privacy of my family if I was writing about home life, and my increasing publication profile, around which I was worried about accidental self-plagiarism (a common concern for doctoral researchers) and visibility of my 'unformed thoughts in progress.' I started to feel increasingly vulnerable about just putting this sketchy, work-in-progress in the public domain. I was also conscious of my own 'newness' in research terms and lacked some confidence in myself as a researcher. The writing helped me to explore some of these emotions and relate them to the theories I was engaging with through my reading. By the end of 2016, I had made the entire blog password protected. As time progressed, I was writing up and then submitting my PhD and I had kind of moved on from the blog, even from doing this kind of writing at all. The blog still exists, however, and contains over 200,000 words of notes, sketches, poems, reflections and citations from a two-year period.

BLOGGING AS REFLECTION ON WRITING

At around the same time that I was exploring writing through my blog, I submitted a short piece of writing to a writing competition I found in a literary journal. The theme was 'the story of us', and contributors were invited to submit 'life writing' or 'memoir' around this topic. Although I had never officially published anything of this kind before, I had been dabbling with autoethnographic writing for my doctorate, which was broadly ethnographically-informed (see Bradley, 2018). My short piece won the first prize and was published in both an anthology and a parenting magazine. I was also interviewed for the publisher's website. This moment – the moment of being published – was quite pivotal in terms of what I had imagined 'being published' would be like and what it actually felt like. I reflected on it in my blog (June 2015):

> Back in December, during the Christmas holidays just as my two-year-old mysteriously became a nocturnal creature, I wrote a little piece of prose and submitted it to a writing competition. It was a memoir, 1,200 words of reflection and musing on the first few months of my eldest daughter's life. These months weren't quite what I expected. At four weeks' old, she was seriously ill, and we spent a week in hospital, with rounds of tests trying to determine what was wrong. The next few months were a blur of feeding, worrying and watching her as she slept. Nothing like they told us at NCT class, that's for sure.

> (*Continued*)
>
> Writing about this experience was easier than I expected, cathartic I suppose. It was over 5 years ago that it happened so I was distant enough from it all to be able to write from a position of knowing that it all worked out ok in the end. But submitting it, finding out I had won and was going to be published in a printed anthology and a magazine, that was hard. I almost withdrew. Encouraged by family and friends, I went ahead with it. I sent it to people to read, almost to dare myself to do it. Like some sort of extreme sport.

Later that year, in October 2015, I came back to this experience in my blog:

> My book (or the anthology in which my tiny piece of writing is being published) is now out, and I'm waiting for my copies. My interview went up on the publisher's blog this week, and I had a minor wobble about the whole thing (as in, that's me, on a website, with a photo (in Keswick), saying things about my story). But now I have decided to just own it, and be a little bit proud. Because proud is exactly how I feel of my friends when they write, take photos, draw and paint and generally create things.
>
> I think about Joan Didion's essay (1976) on why she writes 'In many ways writing is the act of saying I, of imposing oneself upon other people, of saying listen to
>
> (*Continued*)

> (*Continued*)
>
> me, see it my way, change your mind. It's an aggressive, even a hostile act.'
>
> So a blog, or a short story, or a piece of personal writing, or a poem, or a song or any writing at all – it's hostile and aggressive. I can see that. I think partly my little niggle about my story being published is that I feel like I am pushing myself, my thoughts and my words onto people. Especially when it's personal writing of that kind and there's that fear of oversharing or narcissism. A bit like with my blog (although very few people read it and it's mainly for me as a record).

I go on to connect this to a seminar on creative practice and the arts, that I co-organised in October 2015 with a colleague, Lou Harvey, focusing on arts-based research in applied linguistics and intercultural communication.

> Which got me thinking about process and about why I bother to write. It was partly (or even mainly) the seminar yesterday in which people discussed visual methods for research that made me change my mind about publicising my piece of writing. We had presentations using poetry, song, drawing, dramatic inquiry…all wonderfully inspiring. And when I look to my research and to my blog, which is a patchworky repository of some sort, but of which I'm feeling increasingly proud. I have published over 55 posts. That's a lot of (reasonably eclectically diverse) words.

(Continued)

And at yesterday's seminar we talked about purpose. What is the purpose? Why write a poem? Why write anything at all? Why research? And I realised I shift forwards and backwards (side to side and under the table) with this. I *think* that my stance is roughly that purpose isn't always obvious at first. But that purpose often is drawn out through the process. So in terms of my piece of writing, what was the purpose? [...]

So it's a good question. What was the purpose of my 1,200 (technically 1,197) words of prose? It helped me to reflect on something that happened and commit it to a structure (a bit like with the poetry workshop). It helped me articulate it. Actually, it gave me a tiny bit of evidence that my writing is not at all bad. But, it also helped me connect with friends (and with strangers) about this experience which is common. It's about messiness, and life, and chaos, and that awful (and simultaneously liberating) realisation that possibly no-one has the right answers. It was the first time I realised that sometimes doctors don't know what is wrong. And my first real and scary hospital experience. A friend wrote this in an email to me (I don't think she'd mind me publishing it) after reading it: I remember talking to you when you were still in the hospital and crying at my desk afterwards. I'm so sad that you both had to go through that. What was the illness? I don't really remember. I do remember coming to see you in that icy January, and you weren't in a great place emotionally. No surprise – how could you have been?

(Continued)

> (*Continued*)
>
> And then I sent it to an old school friend who's just had her first baby (she asked me to – I did warn her about the content). She said she wanted to read more.
>
> I thought about how much I'd enjoyed reading Rachel Cusk's *A Life's Work* after I'd had E [my youngest daughter] because it was real, and raw, and actually matched the experience.
>
> I then considered what Lou said yesterday about withness and how this fits within that. We write to connect and we write to articulate. We do this through stories. But how does this connect to my research? And ethnography? And writing about people, and places, and how people communicate with each other around stories. Stories formed the core thread of my pilot phase research. B [one of my research collaborators] 'makes visual stories.' And suddenly the fact that the boundaries blur and the borders go backwards and forwards and switch around doesn't seem to matter so much. Because friends read my story and they remembered that time. But they also thought about their own experiences of illness, of having children, of being terrified.

CONCLUSION

Reading these blog posts now, nearly a decade on, I notice how I am labouring to understand the writing process, drawing in examples from across my (wide) reading, conversations with friends and colleagues, emails, and responses to my writing. I am also struck by the circularity. My recent and current research (see Bradley & Pöyhönen, 2024) explores mothers' and birthing parents' individual and collective creative journaling of experience, at the intersections of arts and health. I continue to collaborate with my friend and colleague Lou, whom I mention in the blog post. One of the presenters at the seminar to which I refer is one of the editors of this volume. And in my teaching, in particular at doctoral level, I notice how much I draw on these early experiences of grappling with writing and experience and how glad I am to have these fragments of blog writing which captured a slice of the experience. These early experiences shape our writerly selves, and the things and states we imagine as our writerly futures, foregrounding our uncertainty.

REFERENCES

Allsop, Y., Rzyankina, E., Zhao, S., & Rowsell, J. (2022). Editorial: What shelfies can tell us about pandemic life. *Digital Culture and Education*, *14*(2). https://www.digitalcultureandeducation.com/volume-14-2-papers/allsop-2022. Accessed on July 25, 2024.

Anderson, B. (1983). *Imagined communities: Reflections on the origin and spread of nationalism*. Verso.

Bradley, J. (2015a). The first winter. In T. Bellamy (Ed.), *The mother's milk writing prize anthology 2014: The story of us* (Winner: Prose Category).

Bradley, J. (2015b, June 5). Writing on motherhood: The first winter – Published. *Jessica Mary Bradley*. https://jessicamarybradley.wordpress.com/2015/06/05/published/. [not in public domain].

Bradley, J. (2015c, October 17). Why write? *Jessica Mary Bradley*. https://jessicamarybradley.wordpress.com/2015/10/17/why-write/. [not in public domain].

Bradley, J. (2018). *Translation and translanguaging in production and performance in community arts*. PhD Thesis. University of Leeds.

Bradley, J., & Pöyhönen, S. (2024). Walking with: Understandings and negotiations of the mundane in research. *Applied Linguistics Review*. https://doi.org/10.1515/applirev-2024-0069

Didion, J. (1976, December 5). Why I write. *The New York Times*, 270.

Olusoga, Y., & Bannister, C. (2023). What's behind the mask? Family, fandoms and playful caring around children's masks during the Covid-19 pandemic. In A. Beresin & J. Bishop (Eds.), *Play in a Covid frame. Everyday pandemic creativity in a time of isolation* (pp. 395–426). Open Book Publishers.

Olusoga, Y., & Bradley, J. (2025). Trans-spatial, trans-media flows: Family ethnographies of children's creative exploration of identities in and out of digital space(s). In M. McClure Sweeny & M. Sakr (Eds.), *Postdevelopmental approaches to digital arts in childhood*. Bloomsbury.

6

A GARDEN OF FORKING PHD PATHS

EDD ASPBURY-MIYANISHI

University of Leeds, UK

> In some ways, Edd's story has a similar pattern to many other storytellers in this volume – his Master's studies at The University of Manchester prompted him to continue to doctoral study within the same department. But his story is unusual for this volume in that his doctorate was completed via publication rather than by thesis. Whilst doctorate by publication is increasingly common in the specific university community in which Lantern sits, doctorate by thesis has traditionally been the typical route. Edd's story is also strongly shaped by the COVID-19 pandemic, which dominated so many aspects of life during the years of his doctoral studies. His doctoral completion (2022a) is the most recent of the storytellers, and his post-doctoral trajectory is still in its early stages.

REIMAGINING MY PHD PLANS

The PhD thesis I submitted in 2022 (Aspbury-Miyanishi, 2022a) bears very little resemblance to the one I envisaged in my proposal, back in the halcyon days of early 2019. Indeed, so different are the two documents that it's hard to credit, even as the writer of both, that the one did in fact follow from the other. COVID-19, of course, had a good deal to say in the matter, but I think that is only part of the story. The alternative format of my thesis and the publication process that went with it, coupled with an eminently side-trackable mind probably did as much to doom my proposed plan. Indeed, even if the pandemic had not thrown a mighty spanner into the research works, I think my thesis would still have evolved away from the plan. In this respect, my writing process might be atypical.

A central pillar of my thesis was to be some empirical research into language teachers' intuitive expectations of what happens in 'ordinary' classrooms. In the early days of the pandemic, this was simply postponed, but as the crisis stretched itself out, the prospect of researching 'ordinary' classrooms evaporated. In response, I turned the thesis into a theoretical one and tried to salvage the research concept in the form of a chapter on the proposed. This sounds like something of a catastrophe, and no doubt, for many of my fellow PhD candidates of the same vintage, it probably was. But for me, I must confess I was rather relieved. I was not sure how good my research was really going to be and not being one of life's natural project managers, the thought of carrying out the research – on my own – was rather daunting. Having to knock the thing on the head meant I could focus on theoretical development; something I was much more comfortable with and more motivated to do.

Having to make radical changes to the research in response to COVID-19 was of course nothing unique. However, at the suggestion of my supervisor, I chose to do an alternative format thesis rather than a traditional monograph and my experience doing this is perhaps not so common. The idea was to have five publishable journal article-format chapters, bookended by an introduction and conclusion to tie the articles together. Beyond the main advantage of having something immediately publishable, I found this alternative format cognitively easier to approach. It was easier to write and be motivated to write when I was working on a relatively short, self-contained piece that would actually come to something; that is, it might be published and people might even read it. The thought of chipping away at an 80,000-word saga that only my examiners would actually read would, I fear, have struggled to tap the frustratingly hard-to-find veins of my motivation to write. The desire to get something published also gave me some structure and finality to the chapters – I had at some point to decide the article was finished and submit it somewhere, and I would have to leave the chapter in its published/submitted form. This was the equivalent of putting the biscuit tin on a high, inaccessible shelf to stop myself snacking; once finished, I could no longer go back to the article and waste time incessantly and obsessively tinkering with it.

A THESIS AS AN EVOLVING COLLECTION OF CHAPTERS

I did have a plan for what each chapter was going to address. As I mentioned, one of the chapters was to be the proposed methodology for the research I abandoned. However, this plan also went by the wayside in rather short order. The process of writing and first article and having it reviewed (Aspbury-Miyanishi, 2021) reconfigured what I was interested in and what made sense to write about. This article articulated my new perspective on teacher practical knowledge informed by ecological psychology and phenomenology. One reviewer and my second supervisor both made (somewhat negative) comments about how my model seemed to have no space for teacher agency. The article, which had already ballooned to a 9,000-word megalith in the review process, had no room to address this point. But, if two people had already mentioned agency, I felt I had to respond. I think I rather took the comments as a challenge, and this probably opened up a deep vein of motivation to read and write. I quickly found myself writing a whole new article about agency (Aspbury-Miyanishi, 2022b), a topic I had not even mentioned in my proposal or alternative format outline.

In addition to this impromptu addition, the fact that I was researching for each article individually, rather than reading everything then compiling it into a single text, meant that what seemed logical to write about changed. In the first and second article, I make a passing comment about the positive overlap between my perspective and an approach called 'teacher noticing' – i.e. the ways teachers attend to, and make practical sense of, teaching situations. As I explored this research further, I reworked the third article to address the concept of noticing more directly and this time, more critically. Yet more, following more research, feedback from reviewers on Article 3 and the development of my own thinking, I came back to the concept of noticing in Article 4 (Aspbury-Miyanishi, 2024) with a more tempered perspective and again in the conclusion with an even more agreeable disposition. On top of this, the literature I was reading for this article was quite different to that of the first two, and I decided to drop some of the terminology I had used for the first two articles. Again, the article that emerged was not planned in my original proposal and even took the thesis in a slightly different direction from the trajectory Articles 1 and 2 had set. All I can say is that it seemed to be the right thing to be writing about at the time and at least in my head, was a logical progression.

The fourth and final article (Aspbury-Miyanishi, 2024) came about in much the same way as Article 2 (Aspbury-Miyanishi, 2022b). While writing Article 3, I realised an interesting implication for teacher development was falling out of what I was saying. Once again, I had never planned to address teacher development, but it seemed non-sensical to ignore the implications that had emerged from Article 3. By the time I was working on Article 4, any notion of the thesis tracking what I had planned to do was out the window. The article aimed at salvaging my initial empirical research now made very little sense with the other articles and any motivation to finish it had withered away long ago. The last vestige of this research, which was supposed to be the centrepiece of my thesis, was the pilot study which ended up as an appendix. I was left with four article chapters, not five, of which only the first one vaguely resembled what I had intended to write and even that morphed into something rather different in response to reviewer comments.

LOOKING BACK ON THE WRITING PROCESS

I think I was lucky to have a supervisor who seemed to be as comfortable with spontaneity as I was and was happy to let my interest dictate the direction of my thesis. From the outside, the evolution of my thesis must seem ludicrously haphazard, having no apparent relation to the plan, frequently changing direction on little more than what interested me at the time, inconsistent in terminology and opinion and a less phlegmatic supervisor would probably have had a hard time with me. I can't imagine many traditional monographs and maybe even other alternative format theses that have the same sort of chaotic dragon-walk to their progression.

On reflection, it seems I have a sort of writing myopia. I don't seem capable of planning several steps ahead but rather only know what Step 2 will be about while I'm in the middle of Step 1. The best analogy I can give for this is of mountaineering. From one peak, you think the path before you is going to take you to the summit you can see directly ahead, but when you actually follow the path, you end up climbing a different peak and once there, going to the other peak doesn't seem to make sense anymore. And now, a new path is visible which looks more interesting than the original route you planned and a passing hiker makes an offhand comment about how great the view is from there.

I don't think this as a necessarily bad way of going about the thesis. I think it helped me maintain motivation as I felt compelled to write each article in order to close a loop I opened in the previous article rather than plod through an article because I had planned to do so. Even if there is no obvious linear link from one article to the next, it feels like they are nonetheless exploring the same conceptual space and so make perfect sense to me. I also think it gives my thesis a more organic feel. I like the fact that the evolution of my thought and terminology is visible. I also think that this process made for a better final thesis. Had I been forced to stick to my plan, I have no doubt I would have ended up writing articles trying to answer a question I no longer cared to answer and so at best would have phoned in a boring thesis – a cardinal sin in my eyes – if, that is, I ever raised enough motivation to finish such articles.

I have perhaps presented this way of writing as some sort of ode to spontaneity. But that is not to say the experience was without its difficulties. The sort of motivation that underpins this way of working is ephemeral and very fragile. The motivation to write a whole new article in response to a reviewer comment meant the motivation to finish the current article could slacken and the writing of it then became an unpleasant, almost painful, chore. The motivation came in fits and starts and a deep wellspring of drive to write often inexplicably dried up. For a while, I kept hold of a folder full of articles in various stages of incompleteness as a result. Planning became a rather speculative and often futile activity; I could only hazard a guess at what I might be writing next month or what the shape of the final dissertation would be.

There is also a sense in which one can become a hostage to one's own curiosity. An offhand comment by a reviewer, a tangential question that popped into my head, an intriguing reference in a source could open up a rabbit hole that was very difficult not to dive into and thereby render an afternoon or even a whole day rather unproductive. Sometimes these side-quests turned up some interesting ideas that I could weave back into the thesis, but very often they did not – a realisation that came to me all too late after I had spent an inordinate amount of time trying to shoehorn this new idea into the text.

That said, I am aware that many other students do not enjoy reading and writing and find it difficult even if they are capable of much greater self-discipline than me. I am lucky to enjoy reading-for-writing and writing itself and to have found of way of working and a thesis format that suits my idiosyncrasies. It also seems to have worked in the sense that I submitted and gained my PhD ahead of my fellow candidates and three of the chapters are now published and an admittedly unrecognisable iteration of the other has also been published. And so, despite nothing really going to plan in my PhD, I came out of it more or less where I had intended to be.

REFERENCES

Aspbury-Miyanishi, E. (2021). The skilled teacher: A Heideggerian approach to teacher practical knowledge. *Curriculum Inquiry*, *51*(5), 479–495. https://doi.org/10.1080/03626784.2021.1973336

Aspbury-Miyanishi, E. (2022a). *In the midst of practice: Developing the skilled teacher approach*. PhD Thesis. The University of Manchester.

Aspbury-Miyanishi, E. (2022b). The affordances beyond what one does: Reconceptualizing teacher agency with Heidegger and ecological psychology. *Teaching and Teacher Education*, *113*, 103662. https://doi.org/10.1016/j.tate.2022.103662

Aspbury-Miyanishi, E. (2024). Guided attention as a strategy for developing teacher sight. *Teacher Development*. https://doi.org/10.1080/13664530.2024.2374856

7

PUBLISH, NOT PERISH: DEVELOPING A PURPOSEFUL APPROACH TO DOCTORAL PUBLICATIONS

MAGDALENA ROSTRON

Georgetown University, Qatar

> As with several other storytellers in this volume, Magdalena ('Magda') completed her PhD via 'in-context' (or distance) mode at The University of Manchester (Rostron, 2019). This meant she mostly stayed in her professional context in Qatar where she taught academic English amongst other things, the location where her doctoral fieldwork also took place. She did make regular, quite short visits to the United Kingdom for ad hoc periods of research methods training, face-to-face supervisory support, participation in the local doctoral community and so on. This mode of study takes more time than the onsite, full-time mode, and Magda seemed to enjoy being a student again and having this external link with Manchester.
>
> *(Continued)*

> (*Continued*)
>
> Her published works predate her doctoral studies (e.g., Rostron, 2009), occurred during them (e.g., Rostron, 2014, 2015, 2018), and continued after them (e.g., Rostron, 2023; Rostron & Marcacci, 2020). Whilst writing this chapter, she decided against a simple narrative of her publishing experience and instead tried to distil the writing and publishing wisdom she has accumulated from her own doctoral and publishing experiences and her teaching of academic writing skills in her professional role.

A PhD student is, or will inevitably end up being, a writer, not just any writer but a peer-reviewed and published one. Almost as soon as we embark on a doctoral research journey, we discover that doctoral research is only a part of it. Another, rather vital, part involves sharing our research through writing about it and publishing what we have written. While not a formal requirement, publications from doctoral students are expected or even taken for granted within many academic communities. The pressure to publish starts early on in the process. It continues beyond the viva and successful graduation, at which point it may become almost a habit, gradually losing its hard and stress-inducing initial edge. Thus, it is mainly at the onset that meaningful support and relevant guidance are needed the most, yet are often absent from the student's experience.

WHAT IS TO BE DONE?

How can a new doctoral researcher ensure a relatively smooth and consistent development of their publishing record necessary to complement their maturing doctoral biography? Thinking of this question made me retrace my own first steps as an academic writer, from the almost haphazard initial moves to the final feat of seeing my words printed in a peer-reviewed publication. Based on those experiences, I want to suggest a few simple ideas, which, if applied at the introductory stages of the doctoral journey, should help to decrease stress and pressure while honing our writerly skills, increasing chances of publishing and – last but not least – taking the pain out of writing yet generating a sense of joy instead.

Thomas Mann, who knew a thing or two about writing, is said to have described a writer as a person for whom writing is more difficult than it is for other people (1973/1903). Doctoral or academic writing is quite unlikely ever to reach the stylistic heights or symbolic depths of a literary masterpiece, arguably with some exceptions, for example, Richard Feynman (2002), Steven Pinker (1997) or Edward O. Wilson (2004), but similarly to literature it is a complex, painstaking and time-consuming procedure, which also relies on the author's creativity combined with a rigorous plan of the writing action.

I found out soon enough in my doctoral peregrinations that developing such an approach to publishing academic articles (or book chapters) was essential if I wanted to contribute effectively to my field, advance my research, and gain peer recognition. As it gradually dawned on me, it was also a mini trial-run of the whole doctoral experience, since its stages mirrored the construction of a standard thesis. So, each writing project was in fact a helpful exercise incrementally preparing me for the mammoth task of producing the final thesis.

SERENDIPITY

Despite being an academic composition teacher at the time, I still needed to remind myself of, and utilise for real, the very same principles of academic writing that I was training my students to adopt. The first and perhaps most obvious step was to identify and refine the topic to write about. Ordinarily, this step is assumed to take place during a comprehensive literature review related to our doctoral research. Conventional wisdom has it that, more often than not, a careful exploration of the current state of scholarship will lead to discovering gaps, inconsistencies, new problems emerging in the studied area, whether related to our main doctoral subject matter or branching out of it.

While the above remains true, an uncharted topic may also arise almost accidentally, as a result of a casual conversation with a colleague, reading or watching something seemingly unrelated or maybe a question asked after a presentation at a conference – all of which happened to me at various points. That serendipity (defined by *Oxford Dictionary* as 'an unplanned fortunate discovery') could be a sudden epiphany or a gradual development of thinking about something significant, something that others may have missed. It is partly luck, partly the ability to detect a detail leading to some informational gap in need to be addressed.

In her article *A Key Part of Creativity Is Picking up on What Others Overlook*, Madeleine Gross, a scientist at the University of California, Santa Barbara, states that creative minds tend to spot 'novel or unconventional information' which could explain how scholars work, too:

> *When unconventional information gets flagged, it acts like a magnet, compelling individuals to explore it. This exploration boosts the chances that novel information will become a part of the creative*

> *problem-solving process, sparking innovative ideas.*
> *(Gross, 2024)*

Even though only exceptional individuals will make discoveries comparable to Newton's gravity or Einstein's relativity theories, a dose of this sort of creative alertness can be very fruitful also in (much) smaller-scale scholarly endeavours.

My first topic, compelling me to explore it, emerged from such serendipitous circumstances. A random conversation led me to an article in *The New York Times* (Lewin, 2008) which, in turn, left me with an unanswered question. The question concerned the relevance of liberal arts and the rationale for rejecting them in the specific educational environment where I was teaching and which I was investigating as part of my PhD work. Of course, the initial spark of inspiration was not enough. Only once I aligned my question with relevant methodological and analytical approaches that my thinking started to take more concrete and disciplined shape, transforming itself into academic writing.

WRITING STYLE

It is a truth universally acknowledged that writing becomes easier and more efficient if done in an organised way. Again, as I was beginning to get on with my writing, I found myself referring to the same age-old standards of composition that I had been drilling into my students: notes, organisation, logic, connections and revision. Another point, present in my composition teaching and increasingly clear to me as a writer, was that all the good qualities of a well-written article are enhanced enormously not just by the (presumably) revelatory topic but also by the very writing style. Most readers in this context tend to express a preference for a style characterised by lucidity and succinctness, with a degree of formality, but without the unnecessary jargon, the dreaded 'academese' or a language full of obscure technical terms, stale idioms, overused phrases, etc. Orwell's 'Politics and the English Language,' although published in 1946, is still an unbeatable source of all wisdom on political humbug, which is easily applicable to academic writing.

Yet, this does not mean that academic writing has to be numbingly plain and completely devoid of more figurative, literary language. A skilful metaphor, a valid symbol, a careful rhetorical device (such as a *tricolon*, so beloved of Cicero and Obama) may go a long way towards making our academic prose less turgid but more comprehensible and convincing to the reader. While not always easy or achievable, this is also worth considering while composing academic texts.

GOING FOR PUBLICATION

At some point, the inevitable question arises, where do we take our lovingly crafted manuscript on a fascinating scholarly topic to get it published? Selecting an appropriate journal may seem a daunting task initially, but, in truth, it is made easier by the very fact of our already established, research-related reading pathways. Having pored over hundreds of texts in dozens of journals throughout the doctoral study, we should have some idea which publication is best aligned with our specific research topic and objectives that may have grown out of the broader PhD investigation. Other, more pragmatic, elements to be taken into consideration here are also the journal's scope, audience, impact factor, and acceptance rate. So, having looked around, my choice of an academic journal to try for the first publication was *Intercultural Education*. That choice worked (Rostron, 2009) but not without some initial hurdles.

One of them concerned the journal's submission guidelines, including formatting specifications, word limits, citation style requirements and ethical policies. While mindful of all others, I must admit that I neglected to check what the required citation style was for *Intercultural Education* guidelines, which added extra work as I was forced to reformat the entire text in the correct fashion. Frustratingly, it is still the last thing on my mind when writing a text for publication.

RECEIVING FEEDBACK

Another issue is that an academic article worthy of its name will be peer-reviewed to deem it fit (or not) for publication. The peer review will usually come with critical and detailed evaluation and a request to redraft. Expecting some degree of, hopefully, constructive criticism is the only reasonable attitude to assume. Here, it proved a bit harder than expected for me to follow my own advice to students always to take any feedback in good faith and respond to comments, however scathing, in the best possible way. At first, instead of reworking the draft based on the critical remarks I received, I felt overwhelmed by feelings of inadequacy and ineptitude. But, ultimately, I wanted to get the piece published, so swallowing the bitter pill was the only option. More work, more revision, more rewriting…

Of course, that initial negativity gradually subsided, and later on, with each new article I have submitted for publication, types and amounts of feedback have varied, but each time, it became easier to agree with most or at least some of the recommended modifications. Yes, I would occasionally question and/or reject suggested changes but always with relevant notes for the reviewers to see that their comments were either taken into consideration or dismissed with good justification.

With the draft reviewed and revised, it was ready to go off to the publisher to try again. When I got the final approval, I did have a budding sense of relief and achievement, but my work was still not quite done: there would be the proofs to go over and then some post-publication activities to do with promoting my published work through academic conferences, seminars, workshops, etc., which would in turn pave the way to more publications and invitations to further academic events.

LONE WOLF OR SOCIALLY CONNECTED RESEARCHER?

And this is another key dimension of the path to academic publication, involving a more social approach than the one required by writing, which is normally a solitary activity. A lone wolf of a scholar – even if a genius – needs to leave the comfortable confines of their academic bastille and present their research to the world, with a view to generating attention, interest or inspiration. An essential ingredient of this is a conscious and methodical effort to expand the impact of our research, including participation in events such as local and international conferences, which will ensure exposure to a wider academic community beyond our own doctoral setting. Also known as networking, this kind of exposure can be inspirational as well as leading to more publishing chances, for example by invitation based on our conference papers, presentations or even informal exchanges with fellow participants. It is an ever-widening and ever-shifting cycle of opportunities; all we need to do is spot them and take each one as it comes.

And again, this is exactly what has happened in my case, and not just on one occasion. In fact, at the very beginning of my academic story, it was sharing my informal research (into the issue of culture's impact on students' motivation to learn) that led, via a winding route, indirectly and in stages, not only to related presentations and later on also publications but ultimately to my PhD. It was originally fuelled by a very personal sense of puzzlement as a teacher of English at an Arab university, and at first discussed with just a couple of colleagues, over a cup of coffee in the common office. One of them had connections beyond our institution and encouraged me to follow a contact she suggested.

I did and was offered a slot in a cosy local educational forum where I presented the preliminary findings of my research on the connection between culture and learning motivation. The event brought further interest in my work, the need to deepen and calibrate it and share it with academic audiences in varying places and circumstances. *The New York Times* article (Lewin, 2008) and my first academic publication happened along the same winding route. The rest is history . . .

In conclusion, it is clear that developing a more purposeful and systematic approach to publishing academic articles involves rigorous research, meticulous planning, coherent and readable writing, and strategic dissemination of the published articles or book chapters. Each step, from identifying research gaps to promoting our written work, is crucial in ensuring that our research is impactful and recognised within the scholarly community. Still, what also matters is our readiness to notice and embrace opportunities offered through informal contacts and exchanges as well as fortuitous instances of inspiration coming from unexpected, sometimes haphazard sources. And that serendipity adds quite another dimension to our scholarly work, making it a joyful journey of discovery, instead of dreaded drudgery.

REFERENCES

Feynman, R. P. (2002). The relation of science and religion. In L. A. Jacobus (Ed.), *A world of ideas: essential readings for college writers* (6th ed., pp. 503–516). Bedford/St. Martin's.

Gross, M. (2024, September 19). A key part of creativity is picking up on what others overlook. *Psyche*. https://psyche.co/ideas/a-key-part-of-creativity-is-picking-up-on-what-others-overlook

Lewin, T. (2008, February 11). In oil-rich Mideast, shades of the Ivy League. *The New York Times*. https://www.nytimes.com/2008/02/11/education/11global.html

Mann, T. (1973). Tristan. In H. T. Lowe-Porter (Trans.), *Death in Venice, Tristan, Tonio Kröger*. Penguin. (Original German work published in 1903).

Orwell, G. (1946). Politics and the English language. *Horizon*, *13/76*, 252–265. https://www.orwellfoundation.com/the-orwell-foundation/orwell/essays-and-other-works/politics-and-the-english-language/

Pinker, S. (1997). *How the mind works*. Norton.

Rostron, M. (2009). Liberal arts education in Qatar: Intercultural perspectives. *Intercultural Education*, *20*(3), 219–229.

Rostron, M. (2014). Exploring identity of non-native teachers of English through narratives of their experience. In P. Breen (Ed.), *Cases on teacher identity, diversity, and cognition in higher education* (pp. 140–170). IGI Global.

Rostron, M. (2015). A cultural other in transnational education: Impact of globalization on student and teacher identities. In L. Seawright & A. Hodges (Eds.), *Learning across borders: Perspectives on international and transnational higher education* (pp. 193–215). Cambridge Scholars Publishing.

Rostron, M. (2018). Rethinking critical thinking in a non-western educational context. In M. Rajakumar (Ed.), *Western curricula in international contexts* (pp. 113–132). Lexington Books.

Rostron, M. (2019). *Students' experiences of othering: An ethnographic case study of an English language university preparatory programme in Qatar*. PhD Thesis. The University of Manchester.

Rostron, M. (2023). A reflection on social justice in international EAP: Addressing (or not…) gender inequality through English instruction. In P. Breen & M. le Roux (Eds.), *Social justice in EAP and ELT contexts: Global higher education perspectives* (pp. 177–188). Bloomsbury.

Rostron, M., & Marcacci, R., Jr. (2020). English language poetry and Qatari students. In E. Buscemi & I. Kaposi (Eds.), *Everyday youth cultures in the Gulf peninsula: Changes and challenges* (pp. 217–233). Routledge.

Wilson, E. O. (2004). *On human nature*. Harvard University Press.

COMMENTARY TO PART B

RICHARD FAY[a] AND ACHILLEAS KOSTOULAS[b]

[a]The University of Manchester, UK
[b]University of Thessaly, Greece

The contributions that make up the second part of this collection offer insights into how the writing process is experienced by doctoral students and early career researchers (ECRs). In terms of their scope, they range from reflections on short pieces of writing (Jessica Bradley) to a narrative retelling of a PhD project (Edd Aspbury-Miyanishi) and ultimately to a presentation of insights generated over a longer period of time (Magda Rostron). Their varying timescales and differing orientations notwithstanding, these narratives help us to understand the complexity of the academic writing process, as 'intentional activity', a term borrowed from Stelma and Kostoulas (2021).

Intentional activity, as used here, is an activity that takes place in an ecology, in ways that fuse individual intention, shared meaning-making, meaning sedimented in societal artefacts (i.e., 'derived' meaning; Searle, 1983) and sociocultural expectations. In perhaps the most obvious sense, intentional activity (in this case academic writing) is shaped by the authors' intentions, their knowledge, cognitions, and interests. Edd's statement that he let his 'interest dictate the direction of [his] thesis' illustrates such individual aspects of intentionality well. As Jess points out, however, academic writing is also shaped by interactions with critical friends, mentors, and other members of our immediate community, which give shape not just to texts but also to our imagined writing trajectories. Established expectations about what it means to be 'not just any writer, but a peer-reviewed and published one' (Magda), sometimes sedimented into curricular documents, writing style guides, instructions to the author and the like, are of course also important in shaping the writing experience.

The meaning-structures outlined above, which shape the writing experience, can be configured in different ways to produce different patterns of activity (Stelma & Kostoulas, 2024). Because activity in ecologies is often influenced by its own historicity, the patterns of writing activity can be strongly normative. Magda's contribution, which draws on extensive teaching experience as a writing instructor, suggests how such normative patterns may be operationalised, in the form of sound advice to approach writing in systematic and sustained ways, or by building on a rich history of good writing examples. The other two narratives in the collection, however, both of which are situated in the unprecedented disruption caused by the COVID-19 pandemic, also suggest the potential and promise of creativity, produced when the constraints of historicity are loosened.

It would be injudicious to use the comments above as the basis for an unproductive dichotomy (e.g., between creative and normative modes of writing, between individual and sociocultural aspects of intentionality). An ecological perspective suggests that all of the above are present, in different shapes and to varying degrees, in all types of academic writing. What is perhaps a more productive way forward is to reflect on which dynamics are most suitable to different settings and desired outcomes and manage the resources available to us in order to produce such dynamics.

REFERENCES

Searle, J. R. (1983). *Intentionality: An essay in the philosophy of mind*. Cambridge University Press.

Stelma, J., & Kostoulas, A. (2021). *The intentional dynamics of TESOL*. De Gruyter.

Stelma, J., & Kostoulas, A. (2024). Revisiting complex dynamic systems theory: Empowering language teachers and teaching. *TESOL Journal, 15*(3), e790. https://doi.org/10.1002/tesj.790

though I was hoping for more direct feedback.

Part C

ENGAGING WITH CO-AUTHORS AND CRITICAL PEERS

8

WRITING AND PUBLISHING COLLABORATIVELY: A SAFE SCAFFOLD FOR AN ECR

SITI MASRIFATUL FITRIYAH

University of Jember, Indonesia

> Like Edd (Chapter 6), Siti Masrifatul Fitriyah ('Fitri') is an example of a Lantern member who took her Master's degree (2008–2009) at The University of Manchester and enjoyed it so much that she progressed to doctoral study in the same department (Fitriyah, 2017). Her doctorate used narrative methods, and during her PhD, she was a strong advocate for PGR development regarding narrative methods, leading training workshops and seminars in this area. A key issue for her was the way in which her doctoral studies in a context where publishing was not a requirement, prepared her (or not) for the more 'publish or perish' culture in her home context. Her story also touches upon the common ECR experience of publishing rejection and imposter syndrome. Her experience of collaborative writing has helped her with both of these challenges.

PUBLISHING PRESSURES

Publishing academic papers has long been a means for members of academia to communicate their thinking and the results of their academic studies and explorations. The increasing number of publications, therefore, has often been translated to the increasing scientific capacity of an institution and often a nation, often leading to the 'publish or perish' culture. This has further intensified the already pressuring demand for publications within the academe, for both tenure and early career academia including those still pursuing their doctorate degrees. Many universities require doctoral students to publish academic papers as a compulsory prerequisite for attaining the degree. This is the case in Japan for example (Lijima & Yamaguchi, 2015). In my home context of Indonesia, this was the case (Fry, Lynham, & Tran, 2023), but the regulation has recently been revoked (MECRT, 2023) to give universities greater autonomy and freedom in determining their degree completion prerequisites.

MY EXPERIENCE OF REJECTION

The demand for publication can add more pressure to the already demanding process of doctoral education, and can be 'disastrous' (Becker & Lukka, 2023, p. 13). To a certain extent, this was what I experienced during my doctoral studies. Although the university where I studied for my PhD did not require publications of academic papers in the academic journals, for early career researchers (ECRs) like me who opted to write a thesis for the completion of the study, the pressure was still on. The pressure to publish in reputable journals stemmed not only from the demand from my sponsor to include the publication progress in every doctoral progress report that I sent them but also from the publication achievements of the people in my circle, from my colleagues and fellow doctoral students both in my university and in other universities including those pursuing their studies in my home country. Being inexperienced in the world of academic publications, I remember how downhearted I felt when my article submissions were rejected, and this, to a certain extent, escalated my anxiety levels as well as my symptoms of impostor syndrome (Fitriyah, 2021), my feeling that I was not equal to my colleagues in terms of what they can achieve and not equal to them intellectually (Hermann, 2016). In addition, the introduction in 2016 of SINTA (the Indonesian database to index and rank researchers from all universities and research institutes in Indonesia) in 2016 further intensified the concern. Although the database has been seen as useful to boost the productivity of Indonesian researchers and to improve the overall scientific capacity (Fry, Lynham, & Tran, 2023), the ranking system can be daunting, although also motivating, for ECRs such as myself at that time.

MY EXPERIENCE OF MENTORED SUCCESS

Therefore, I was really excited when one of my mentors invited me to be part of a collaborative writing team and delighted when this resulted in an alphabetically-listed multi-authored publication (Arkhipenka et al., 2018). Being inexperienced in the complicated world of academic publications, I felt really fortunate to have this opportunity, particularly after those earlier rejections from journals which had, to a certain extent, affected my confidence. At the outset of the collaboration, I did not feel at ease and was always nervous during the meetings. From my perspective, it felt like I was unable to contribute significantly to the progress of the research. For instance, when my teammates and I brainstormed the questions of our research instruments, I only managed to contribute two or three sentences to the 24 needed. While two or three sentences might actually be sufficient considering that there were six of us in the team, my overthinking self worried that I was not significantly contributing to the research process. However, as the project proceeded, I became more comfortable and was able to contribute a little more to the team.

Reflecting on the above experience, there were several reasons that I believe may have contributed to my progress and positive feelings of working with the team and eventually to contribute to the publication endeavour. First, the division of writing loads into smaller portions made the task more achievable and made me more confident to finish the particular portion assigned to me. Second, the non-judgemental collaborative environment helped me feel better about working in the team. The team provided all the members with a lot of freedom to express ourselves, to offer what we thought we could do best for our team, to make mistakes, to correct the mistake and to learn from it. An instance was that in our regular discussions to plan and evaluate how we implemented the plan, all the members had the opportunity to report on what they had done to the team who then provided feedback supportively such as regarding the research design, methods and techniques that we used. If we needed it, team members also provided more resources regarding the theoretical framework and any other element of the paper. The opportunity to have fruitful discussions and to learn from each other in a safe environment was very useful for an ECR such as myself and probably my other fellow novice teammates. This safe environment acted as both a space for development and as a scaffold for us novice researchers to challenge ourselves to improve our skills and knowledge.

Another instance was when I offered myself to find a potential journal for our paper and everyone allowed me to. Our submission was rejected by the first journal that I had chosen because it was not in line with their aims and scope. However, no one blamed me or showed any trace of disappointment regarding my choice. Rather, my teammates let me choose another journal, which then I examined more carefully to check the suitability of our paper's theme in relation to the journal's aims and scope. This time we received a positive response from the journal which accepted and published our paper. This process helped me build more trust with my teammates and lessened my feeling of anxiety when working with them, thus helping me feel more relaxed which in turn helped me with a better flow of ideas.

The supportive and respectful teammates may have also played an important role in this regard. One example of this was when we decided on the order of the authors' names in the article listing in the journal. To show appreciation and respect for all members of the team, we adopted alphabetical order, thus avoiding the sense of dominance from any member of the team. However, from my perspective, it would also be acceptable if the order was decided based on some prior agreement among all the members, the agreement helping to avoid a conflict of interests within the team. This alternative may also exemplify a sense of support and respect for the team members and an acknowledgement of their contributions.

Another instance which shows how supportive my teammate, in my point of view, was the fact that most of the sentences that I wrote for my portion were left the way they were without any major changes. Thus, when my 'English native speaker' colleague had done the proofreading on the paper, apart from the few feedback for revisions that I happily received from her, my wording was as I had originally phrased it. As an international student, I was often not confident about my English academic writing skills and was often worried that my sentences would sound 'eccentric' for the readers. Therefore, such a seemingly trivial matter was very meaningful for me, helping me feel more confident about my writing, helping me eventually to write more. Upon reflection, for me, the support and trust I experienced in this collaborative, mentored project helped me gained more confidence in contributing to publication endeavours.

TAKING STOCK

The publication of my first collaborative paper has significantly contributed to my academic journey and taught me the value of collaboration in the incessantly demanding academic world. This successful collaborative publication endeavour, to a certain extent, has helped me feel more confident about being part of the academe. The experience has also inspired me to undertake similar endeavours for academic publications through which I managed to publish more co-authored academic papers. It has also taught me about the publication process, such as how to prepare the cover letter and other supplementary documents, how to cope with rejections, how to respond the reviewers' feedback and make revisions and how to write a piece of publishable academic paper as a whole. This experience provided little steps to scaffolded my improving my publication knowledge and skills which I consider an important milestone in my academic publication journey.

From the experience, I understand that writing an academic paper collaboratively may lessen the burden as members of the team are only responsible for a particular portion of the work. More importantly, the supportive non-judgemental environment, both academically and psychologically, that team members create can provide a sense of comfort and confidence which helps enable all members to significantly contribute to the piece of academic work, and this involvement by all often makes the work more robust, thus improving the chances of it being accepted for publication.

REFERENCES

Arkhipenka, V., Dawson, D., Fitriyah, S., Goldrick, S., Howes, A., & Palacios, N. (2018). Practice and performance: Changing perspectives of teachers through collaborative enquiry. *Educational Research*, *60*(1), 97–112.

Becker, A., & Lukka, K. (2023). Instrumentalism and the publish-or-perish regime. *Critical Perspectives on Accounting*, *94*, 102436. https://doi.org/10.1016/j.cpa.2022.102436

Fitriyah, S. M. (2017). *Experiencing policy change and reversal: Indonesian teachers and the language of instruction*. PhD Thesis. The University of Manchester.

Fitriyah, S. M. (2021). Surviving impostor syndrome: Navigating through the mental rollercoaster of a doctoral sojourn. *Journal of International Students*, *12*(2). https://doi.org/10.32674/jis.v12i2.3274

Fry, C. V., Lynham, J., & Tran, S. (2023). Ranking researchers: Evidence from Indonesia. *Research Policy*, *52*(5), 104753. https://doi.org/10.1016/j.respol.2023.104753

Herrmann, R. (2016). *Impostor syndrome is definitely a thing*. The Chronicle of Higher Education.

Lijima, H., & Yamaguchi, E. (2015). Decrease in the number of journal articles in Physics in Japan. Correlation between the number of articles and doctoral students. *Journal of Integrated Creative Studies*, 1–20. https://www2.yukawa.kyoto-u.ac.jp/~future/icis/archives/category/backnumber?id=en

Minister of Education, Culture, Research and Technology (MECRT) of the Republic of Indonesia. (2023). *Salinan Peraturan Menteri Pendidikan, Kebudayaan, Riset, dan Teknologi Republik Indonesia Nomor 53 Tahun 2023 tentang Penjaminan Mutu Pendidikan Tinggi*. The Ministry of Education, Culture, Research and Technology of the Republic of Indonesia. https://jdih.kemdikbud.go.id/sjdih/siperpu/dokumen/salinan/salinan_20230829_094323_Salinan%20Permen%2053%20Tahun%202023%20JDIH.pdf

9

THE BENEFITS OF 'BEING SHAPED' AS AN EARLY CAREER RESEARCHER

DYLAN WILLIAMS

Queen Mary University of London, UK

Dylan is another of the pioneering 'in-context' (i.e., distance learning mode at Manchester) doctoral students who embarked upon his PhD (Williams, 2020) having previously enjoyed a distance learning mode MA TESOL programme in the same department. His research, and related publishing agenda, highlights a desire for his work to have contextual relevance, a concern echoing the earlier stories by Made (Chapter 3) and Magda (Chapter 7). His story of transformation (regarding the appreciation of what publishing involves) is one that had to deal with rejection before achieving success with a mix of solo-authored (e.g., Williams, 2022) and collaborative writing with his supervisor (Williams & Stelma, 2022).

RESEARCHING MY PROFESSIONAL WORLD

In the two-year period following my viva, I was still living and working in South Korea, where I had conducted my research into Higher Education students' perceptions of English Medium Instruction (EMI), and was immersed in a real-world environment where the practical implications of my research could be directly observed. From this situatedness, I felt a strong responsibility to share my findings with a broader audience. This unique position allowed me to see firsthand the challenges and opportunities within my area of study, further igniting my passion to influence positive change through knowledge dissemination. By publishing my research, I aimed to bridge the gap between theory and practice, providing valuable insights that could inform policy, guide future research and enhance professional practices around the area of EMI in the Asian higher education context. In this sense, I felt my research could help to make students' learning experiences more socially just, which to me was an important endeavour. Additionally, contributing to the academic community through publications was, I felt, a way to validate the significance of my work, ensuring that my research not only added to the existing body of knowledge but also addressed pertinent issues faced by practitioners and stakeholders in my field. This commitment to making a tangible impact was the driving force behind my efforts to share my research findings through various academic and professional channels.

PUBLISHING FROM THE PHD

Within two years of submitting my PhD thesis, two of my papers had been accepted for publication. One, a collaborative effort with my main supervisor (Williams & Stelma, 2022), was accepted by the journal *Teaching in Higher Education* for a special issue titled 'Critical Perspectives on Teaching in the Multilingual University.' The other was a solo-authored paper that has found a home in the *ELT Journal* (Williams, 2022). Reaching this stage of positive outcomes has not been without its challenges. The journey from the initial aspiration to publish my research to seeing my work accepted involved numerous rejections, revisions, and a significant amount of perseverance. Nevertheless, this 'steep-learning curve' proved invaluable in shaping me in my quest to be published.

From my experiences, I would advise other early career researchers (ECRs) that want to develop their publishing profiles to take advantage of any publishing opportunities that may come their way that may not be tied to prestigious journals. My first experience with publishing came at the end of my Master's programme. I managed to get my MA dissertation published in a lower-ranked journal (Williams, 2011). Then in the early stages of my PhD training I also managed to get a paper published in a lower-ranked journal, which was based upon research I had conducted for one of the requisite modules I undertook as part of my PhD studies (Williams, 2016). Additionally, as I was writing the literature review for my PhD thesis, on the advice of my supervisor, I published a systematic literature review (Williams, 2015) again in a lower-ranked journal. However, the impact of this paper has been significant as it has, to date, been cited 75 times according to Google Scholar. What I realise from this experience is that the content of your paper may sometimes carry more weight than the journal outlet it is published in. For me, writing a paper based on smaller projects was a valuable introduction to the publishing process and I feel helped me tackle more prestigious journals later on. Thus, embracing these initial publishing opportunities provided me with some crucial experience and paved the way for future success.

SHAPING EXPERIENCES

Another experience which greatly shaped me as an early career researcher was the mentoring experience I received from my first supervisor as we collaborated on co-authoring a paper for a special issue (Williams & Stelma, 2022). During my PhD journey, we had at times contemplated the idea of co-authoring a future publication based on some insights that had emerged from my thesis, and this special issue seemed the perfect opportunity to do so. I benefited from this experience is several ways as it made the journey of writing the paper less isolating and more enriching. This is because my supervisor brought his extensive knowledge and experience to the research project, which provided me with an opportunity for learning and mentorship. As our collective thinking was maturing throughout the process of writing and developing our paper, our collective critical thinking was enhanced by sharing our diverse perspectives and critiques which were brought to the surface through our own discussions and through ongoing feedback from the series editors.

From this collaborative experience, I feel that it helped accelerate my professional growth and helped to shape me as a credible and capable researcher. Ultimately, this experience helped to build my confidence. Particularly, I gained enhanced insights into the intricacies of academic writing which have helped me to approach future research papers with a more coherent line of argumentation throughout and with more rigour to the persuasive aspects to help make it more appealing to reviewers. Also, through collaborating, I gained valuable input on how to respond to reviewer comments and manage revisions.

Upon reflection, I feel that the combination of innovative ideas stemming from my thesis and the refined judgement and experience of my supervisor in better articulating them led to a higher-quality paper. Overall, my experience of co-authoring with my supervisor enhanced the quality of my research, provided a valuable learning experience, and supported my career development. This is because one of the editors of the special issue invited me to co-convene a research network that has recently been approved by the Research and Development Committee of the Society for Research in Higher Education. Moreover, on account of the success of the special issue, the paper is now published as a chapter in a book (Williams & Stelma, 2024). Overall, my experience of being shaped by my PhD supervisor as an ECR has fostered my holistic development that encompasses my academic, professional and personal growth.

Advice I received during my viva for publishing from my PhD thesis proved crucial in providing me with publishing goals to aim for. My examiners, experts who had meticulously read my entire thesis, enquired into my plans of publishing and through the ensuing discussion suggested several potential papers that could be derived from my research and recommended journals that might be suitable for these papers. This guidance was instrumental. Within the first year after my viva, I had drafted all three suggested papers and began to submit to potential journals in the hope of getting published.

DEALING WITH REJECTIONS

I soon discovered that the exhilaration of submitting a paper was not long after tempered by the reality of the academic publishing world. From experiencing a few rejections, I discovered that publishing work as an ECR presented several challenges. As I now reflect upon this time, my limited publishing experience often made me feel as though I was 'feeling around in the dark'. Perhaps, in my initial introduction to the publishing realm, I was being too ambitious by aiming to get my work published in high-profile (SSCI Q1) journals where competition is intense and involves competing for space with seasoned researchers with established reputations. Additionally, due to my limited experience with the publication process, upon reflection, I may not, at the time, have identified the most appropriate journals for my work.

From this experience, I would advise other ECRs aiming to publish to do your 'homework'. This involves ensuring your paper fits the journal's aims and scope, emulating the organizational and writing style of previously published papers and paying close attention to referencing and citation conventions. It is also crucial to clearly articulate your paper's unique contribution to the field. A useful exercise I found to achieve this outcome was writing brief replies to questions such as 'What is your paper's unique selling point?' and 'How does it fit the aims and scope of the journal?' Replies to these questions helped me to refine the focus of my paper and prepare a more compelling submission. Through this process, I was able to identify the original insights that my paper offered and highlight the relevancy of a paper's topic to current issues in my research field as well as highlight how it connects with ongoing discussions and contributes to future developments.

The above process helped me to refine my thinking as I was able to clarify the paper's focus. In doing so, I was able to eliminate unnecessary content and focus more on the core contributions. I was also able to home in more on the purpose of the paper, ensuring that every section supports the unique value proposition. Moreover, the process helped to strengthen my argument as it helped me ensure that the logic throughout the paper leads to a more coherent and convincing argument. To further help refine thinking, I would also advise ECRs about the importance of sharing work with critical readers prior to submission and the importance of writing multiple drafts to help clarify thoughts and ideas. Critical readers can bring new perspectives to the paper through objective viewpoints and help address the structure and readability of the paper.

Nevertheless, despite thorough preparation, I have discovered that rejection is a common part of the publishing process. While it can be disheartening, I found it important to view rejection as an opportunity for growth and to be shaped by the process. Reviewers' comments, though sometimes tough to hear, provided valuable insights that helped strengthen my submitted papers. Throughout the process, I found it imperative to develop a 'thick skin' and not take critique personally but rather constructively. For me, taking critique constructively rather than personally involves adopting a mindset and approach that focuses on growth, improvement and objectivity rather than on emotional reactions or self-defence. In other words, I view critique as a 'tool' for improving my writing and ideas. A growth mindset is therefore imperative to view critique as an opportunity to provide valuable insights that can guide development.

CONCLUDING REMARKS

In sum, though the fruits of my labour took time to materialise, I now realise that every interaction with editors and reviewers has contributed to shaping me as a researcher and writer. From my experiences, I would advise other ECRs to embrace the journey and let each experience inform and enhance your academic development.

Upon reflection, embarking on the journey from doctoral graduation to achieving my post-doctoral publications in what are considered prestigious outlets has been a transformative experience, replete with challenges and learning opportunities. It has been an intricate process of academic growth which made me realise that writing papers in SSCI Q1 academic oriented publications demands much rigorous thought and effort. The process has been a steep learning curve to me that shaped my development as a researcher, highlighting the critical importance of perseverance, collaboration and the iterative process of writing and revision. It was through these experiences, particularly the collaborative effort with my main supervisor on a significant journal submission, that I truly began to understand the complexities and rewards of academic authorship.

REFERENCES

Williams, D. G. (2011). Evaluating the L1 Use of adult intermediate Korean English language learners during collaborative oral tasks. Master's Thesis. *Asian EFL Journal*. https://www.asian-efl-journal.com/thesis/evaluating-the-l1-use-of-adult-intermediate-korean-english-language-learners-during-collaborative-oral-tasks/index.htm

Williams, D. G. (2015). A systematic review of EMI and implications for the South Korean higher education context. *ELT World Online*, 1–23. https://blog.nus.edu.sg/eltwo/2015/04/27/a-systematic-review-of-english-medium-instruction-emi-and-implications-for-the-south-koreanhigher-education-context-2/

Williams, D. G. (2016). Understanding the interplay between context and agency in a South Korean high school English classroom. *TESOL International Journal*, *11*(1), 15–32.

Williams, D. G. (2020). Situated linguistic capital: Theorising South Korean higher education students' perceptions of trust in English-Medium instruction. PhD Thesis. The University of Manchester.

Williams, D. G. (2022). Trust and translanguaging in English-Medium instruction (EMI). *ELT Journal*, 77(1), 23–32. https://doi.org/10.1093/elt/ccac016

Williams, D. G., & Stelma, J. (2022). Epistemic outcomes of English medium instruction in a South Korean higher education institution. *Teaching in Higher Education*, 27(4), 453–469. https://doi.org/10.1080/13562517.2022.2049227

Williams, D. G., & Stelma, J. (2024). Epistemic outcomes of English medium instruction in a South Korean higher education institution. In I. Bhatt, K. Badwan, & M. Madiba (Eds.), *Critical perspectives on teaching in the multilingual university* (1st ed., pp. 29–45). Routledge.

10

MY SUCCESSFUL AND LESS SUCCESSFUL PUBLICATION EXPERIENCES

SUTRAPHORN TANTINIRANAT

Burapha University, Thailand

> Sutraphorn Tantiniranat, otherwise known as Khwan, completed her PhD at The University of Manchester (Tantiniranat, 2017). Although she published an e-chapter during her doctoral studies (Tantiniranat, 2015), her portfolio of work (e.g., Sahrai & Tantiniranat, 2024; Tantiniranat, 2020; Tantiniranat & Fay, 2018; Tantiniranat, Fitriyah, & Pérez Gracia, 2024), has largely developed in the years since graduation. In her story, she reflects on some of the positive influences that shaped her early career researcher (ECR) path to publishing, including mentorship and support from experienced colleagues. She also reflects on some of the challenges she faced, such as self-doubt, navigating the complexities of co-authoring with peers and dealing with the intricacies of academic publishing during and after doctoral studies.

PUBLISHING DURING THE PHD

Although there is no formal publication requirement for PhD students at The University of Manchester, I managed to achieve a publication during my doctoral studies. My journey into the world of academic publishing began with my involvement in conferences. Attending and presenting at conferences became an integral part of my practice as a PhD student at Manchester.

My then supervisor and now life-long mentor played a vital role in this process. He introduced me to the academic conference world, providing invaluable guidance and encouragement. Under his mentorship, I gained the confidence to engage with the academic community through these conferences.

In 2015, at a post-graduate studies conference at Cambridge University, I reached a significant milestone in my academic journey. I presented part of my PhD work, and to my delight, my paper was selected to be published in a journal volume dedicated to the conference (Tantiniranat, 2015). Being chosen gave me a sense of validation of the quality of my research. This experience also provided me with first-hand exposure to the peer review process, a critical aspect of academic publication. Receiving feedback from reviewers helped me to see my work from different perspectives and contributed to refining my PhD project.

PUBLISHING EFFORTS TOWARDS THE END OF THE PHD

Following my initial success in getting published (see above), my supervisor extended an exciting and prestigious opportunity to me: the chance to lead a co-authored book chapter. The chapter, entitled *Adding an Interculturally-oriented ELF Dimension to the EFL Classroom in Thai Universities* (Tantiniranat & Fay, 2018), was in a volume edited by Nicos Sifakis and Natasha

Tsantila and published by the respected publisher Multilingual Matters. This opportunity was particularly significant because I could contribute to the field of English as a Lingua Franca (ELF) by sharing part of my PhD studies from the perspective of Thailand's English language teaching. What made this experience even more extraordinary was the calibre of the fellow contributors. The book features chapters by key, pioneering figures in ELF (e.g., Seidlhofer & Widdowson, 2018), whose work I have admired and cited in my research. Working on this book chapter was an enriching experience that broadened my understanding of the process of drafting, revising and finalising the chapter as well as developing my academic writing skills and deepening my expertise in the subject matter. I consider myself fortunate to be part of this volume, and of course, it would not have been possible without the support and guidance from my supervisor.

In 2016, I had the privilege of collaborating on a research study with two remarkable colleagues: a visiting researcher from Spain (Elisa) and my PhD best friend from Indonesia (Fitri). Our study explored the shaping influences of English language curricula in three contexts: Indonesia, Spain, and Thailand. The project was mentored by my supervisor, and we creatively named ourselves KEF(R), an acronym combining the initials of chosen names.

We had the opportunity to present our findings in-house at our university. Building on this, we presented our work at CULTNET, a prestigious network of researchers with a special interest in intercultural communication hosted by Durham University. Despite the progress we made in our research and our presentations, the article we co-wrote on that project seemed never to have been completed. Various factors, including the demands of our individual projects, geographical distances, and personal issues contributed to the difficulties in bringing the manuscript to completion.

PUBLISHING AFTER THE PHD

After my graduation in 2017, I have continued to publish my own work and present my papers at conferences (e.g., Tantiniranat, 2019). I also maintain collaboration with my colleagues (e.g., Sahrai & Tantiniranat, 2024). However, despite holding a PhD, I still have self-doubt and occasionally struggle with imposter syndrome. Nevertheless, I have continued to publish regularly, with at least one paper per year.

In September 2021, an exciting yet unexpected opportunity arose for my Manchester alumni friends and me. We were invited to co-write a book chapter on developing students' intercultural competence through telecollaboration (Tantiniranat, Fitriyah, & Busra, 2023). The project came about quite suddenly, as the editor of the volume was urgently seeking contributors to fill a chapter that was abandoned by other authors. The chance to contribute to this book was too valuable to pass up even though we knew it would require us to work within a tight timeframe. As we began to write, it became clear that there were several challenges to navigate. One of which is who would take the lead on the project. We had to engage in open and honest discussions about our strengths, availability, and how we could best support each other in this collaborative effort. Another challenge was determining the extent of each co-author's contribution. Given the short timeframe, dividing work fairly and efficiently was crucial. The experience reinforced the importance of flexibility, mutual respect, and clear communication in collaborative academic work.

For the KEF(R) paper that seemed never to have been completed, KEF decided to resurrect the manuscript draft we started back in 2016. As time passed, it became increasingly challenging to revisit the project despite our enthusiasm and commitment. Life's demands, professional obligations, and different time zones made it difficult to maintain the momentum, we had when we started the project in Manchester. In particular, each time we returned to work on it, we found ourselves having to re-read and discuss the points we had intended to address ages ago. We felt like a continuous cycle of starting over, and more importantly, the passage of time had made our data and literature review outdated. This posed a significant challenge: we had to conduct a new literature review to identify the latest developments in the field and incorporate more current data and analysis. On many occasions, I thought to myself that it would be easier to begin a new project from scratch rather than attempt to resurrect this one. There were moments of doubt whether the effort would be worth it in the end.

After several unsuccessful attempts over the past few years, we finally succeeded in completing it. After being rejected by a journal, we found a suitable home for our article (Tantiniranat, Fitriyah, & Pérez Gracia, 2024) in *Research in Comparative and International Education*, a well-regarded (Q2) Scopus-indexed journal. This achievement was a testament to our perseverance and strength of collaboration. I feel especially thankful to Fitri, who never gave up on the project and was instrumental in pushing us to submit our work to a decent journal. Looking back, the experience taught me valuable lessons about resilience, teamwork, and the long journey that academic publications can take.

CONCLUSION

Reflecting on my publication journey from a PhD student to ECR, the most crucial aspect has always been the support I received during my doctoral studies. Although it might seem modest when compared to the experiences of other highly successful PhD students, I always appreciate the training and opportunities that were afforded to me. I owe much of my publication success to the unwavering support and mentorship of my supervisor, who believed in my potential and provided the encouragement and guidance needed to navigate the complexities of contributing to academia. His mentorship has had a lasting impact on my academic journey, shaping my approach to research and collaboration.

As an ECR who sometimes self-doubts her ability, to address this, I seek feedback and collaboration from peers and mentors. Nevertheless, self-reliance and academic independence are essential traits I need to develop further. My supervisor once said he was pleased when I did not need his assistance while we presented our paper at a conference, emphasising that a supervisor should ultimately be dispensable. Alongside peer support, I also reflect on past achievements no matter how small they may seem.

Another important aspect of my publication journey is the sense of belonging within the research community. The more I engaged in academic and research communities, the more I developed my identity and felt I was growing as a researcher. This sense of belonging was invaluable as I navigated the complexities of collaboration, which involved fine-tuning theoretical stances, understanding varying degrees of commitment and determining leadership roles. Embracing these challenges not only enhanced my collaborative skills but also provided opportunities for growth.

In my role as a lecturer and academic advisor for MA students, I have co-authored papers with both colleagues (e.g., Olson, Tantiniranat, McHarg, & Carmesak, 2021; Tantiniranat, Treesorn, Boonla, & Warawudhi, 2023) and MA advisees (e.g., Li & Tantiniranat, 2023; Sahrai & Tantiniranat, 2024) and guided them in conference presentations and publications, drawing on the training I received during my doctoral studies.

Some of my colleagues at Burapha University have noted that I am an active member of the academic community there. I owe this to the support of my supervisors and the staff members at the Manchester Institute of Education (MIE), who facilitated documentation on conference funding opportunities. Finally, regardless of my level of success, I am committed to sharing these experiences and offering my assistance to my students and my colleagues who may benefit from it.

REFERENCES

Li, J., & Tantiniranat, S. (2023). Exploring the virtual linguistic landscape of Chinese university websites: A focus on internationalization and multilingualism. *Journal of English Language and Linguistics*, 4(2), 62–80.

Olson, M., Tantiniranat, S., McHarg, M., & Carmesak, W. (2021, Spring). Design and implementation of the first peer-staffed writing center in Thailand. *Composition Forum*, 46. https://compositionforum.com/issue/46/thailand.php

Sahrai, A., & Tantiniranat, S. (2024). "My accent is not okay": Exploring Thai students' attitudes towards English accents. *THAITESOL Journal*, 37(1), 156–178.

Seidlhofer, B., & Widdowson, H. (2018). ELF for EFL: A change of subject? In N. Sifakis & N. Tsantila (Eds.), *English as a lingua franca for EFL contexts* (pp. 17–31). Multilingual Matters.

Tantiniranat, S. (2015). Some intercultural implications of ASEAN and Thai educational policies for Thai higher education. *Cambridge Open-Review Educational Research e-Journal*, 1(2), 154–165.

Tantiniranat, S. (2017). *TESOL purposes and paradigms in an intercultural age: Practitioner perspectives from a Thai university*. PhD Thesis. The University of Manchester.

Tantiniranat, S. (2019). Stars & Stripes and Union Jack: Exploring the presence of native-speaker cultures in an English major program. *Journal of Language and Culture, 38*(2), 202–221.

Tantiniranat, S. (2020, March). Policy direction for Thai English language education in an ASEAN era: Aspirations vs reality. In *2nd International Conference on Education and Social Science Research (ICESRE 2019)* (pp. 253–257). Atlantis Press.

Tantiniranat, S., & Fay, R. (2018). Adding an interculturally-oriented ELF dimension to the EFL classroom in Thai universities. In N. Sifakis & N. Tsantila (Eds.), *English as a lingua franca for EFL contexts* (pp. 72–92). Multilingual Matters.

Tantiniranat, S., Fitriyah, S. M., & Busra, D. A. (2023). Developing ASEAN students' intercultural competence through a telecollaboration program. In F. J. Leandro & R. Oberoi (Eds.), *Disentangled vision on higher education: Preparing the generation next* (pp. 481–495). Peter Lang.

Tantiniranat, S., Fitriyah, S. M., & Pérez Gracia, E. (2024). Disentangling the complexities of English language education policies in diverse contexts: A comparative study. *Research in Comparative and International Education, 19*(1), 112–130. https://doi.org/10.1177/17454999241229650

Tantiniranat, S., Treesorn, P., Boonla, P., & Warawudhi, R. (2023). Exploring English language courses on the Thai MOOC platform. *Academic Journal of Humanities and Social Sciences Burapha University, 31*(2), 62–75.

COMMENTARY TO PART C

RICHARD FAY[a] AND ACHILLEAS KOSTOULAS[b]

[a]The University of Manchester, UK
[b]University of Thessaly, Greece

In the first part of the volume, we looked in the construction of academic identities, and then Part B discussed the construction of academic texts. We also saw how the interaction between the two produces what Jessica Bradley (Chapter 5, p. 58) termed the 'writerly identities'. Part C picks up on this theme, by examining how the writerly identity of doctoral students and early career researchers (ECRs) was shaped by interactions with co-authors and critical peers. Using the vocabulary introduced in the commentary on Part B, these are examples of shared intentionality (Stelma & Kostoulas, 2021). This is the kind of joint meaning-making that occurs in small-group interaction, such as a group of co-authors. The narratives in Part C, which are authored from the perspective of academics who were relatively junior at the time, usefully illustrate how the experience of writing with more established peers shaped both the papers and their own identities as emerging scholars.

In addition to that, however, the narratives in Part C by Siti Masrifatul Fitryah ('Fitri'), Dylan Williams and Sutraphorn ('Khwan') Tantiniranat also usefully exemplify how their emergent 'writerly identities' came into being by synthesising the resources, expectations, opportunities and other meaning-structures in their academic context. Fitri uses the apt metaphor of 'scaffolding' to describe how the practices and attitudes in her author group helped to nurture her academic becoming. Dylan also explicitly discusses the experience of being 'shaped' as a 'credible and capable researcher' (p. 121) through his supervisor's and co-authors' mentoring, the examiners' input after his viva and reviewer feedback. Khwan's narrative also shows how a network of peers helped her identity and act on publishing opportunities and provided her with affective and practical support.

Together, these three narratives demonstrate another aspect of the structure–agency relationship: namely, that the increasingly agentic behaviour of doctoral students and ECRs is the emergent product of interactions with peers and more knowledgeable others. This has implications both for professional development (e.g., it hints at the need to develop dense professional networks) and for mentorship – both formal and informal – by reminding us of the impact our actions have on others.

REFERENCE

Stelma, J., & Kostoulas, A. (2021). *The intentional dynamics of TESOL*. De Gruyter.

Part D

BUILDING OR JOINING AN ACADEMIC COMMUNITY

11

DEVELOPING RESEARCHERHOOD AND PROFESSIONAL BELONGING THROUGH PUBLICATION

ZHUO MIN HUANG

The University of Manchester, UK

Chinese-born Zhuo Min Huang is currently a Senior Lecturer in Education at The University of Manchester. She undertook her postgraduate studies in the United Kingdom culminating with her PhD in Education (Huang, 2019). Hers is a story of notable publishing productivity, with works (see references at the end of the chapter) written during and from her doctorate studies, as focused both directly and less directly about her PhD topic and methodology, and as produced both individually and collaboratively. During her PhD, she led a collaboratively written article (Huang, Fay, & White, 2017) exploring a concept (mindfulness) which was then becoming a key conceptual aspect of her research. This led to a productive

(*Continued*)

> (*Continued*)
>
> line of collaborative work, with her supervisor and other colleagues, capturing an activist researcher stance less directly tied to her doctorate but of great importance to her as an early career academic based in a context in which English is foregrounded.
>
> Min's narrative is one of 'becoming' within an academic community. In it, she illustrates how her early publications were prompted by opportunities that were present in her academic community. However, in addition to identifying an affordance for publishing, her publication success also involved positioning herself in a set of dynamics which were also shaped by considerations of nationality, language, gender and seniority. As Min's 'researcherhood' (Barnard, 2019) developed, the dynamics of her academic environment kept reconfiguring themselves in ways that made possible a large number of single-authored publications and co-authored projects where she had even more prominent roles.

DEVELOPING RESEARCHERHOOD

In this narrative, I reflect on my experience of developing researcherhood and professional belonging through publication from my PhD study to an early-career stage. I use the term 'researcherhood' to refer to an individual's construct of being and becoming a researcher as part of one or more communities. According to Barnard (2019), 'researcherhood' synthesises the need for distinctiveness (e.g., individual identity, voices, expressions) as well as professional belonging and emphasises communication and dialogues with peer researchers in a specific field and solidarity with colleagues in research communities. This understanding provides a starting point for me to reflect on how I have used publication to develop my researcherhood and professional belonging from and beyond my PhD study. Below, I reflect on my first publication during the PhD and my endeavours of publishing from and beyond the PhD.

MY FIRST PUBLICATION

I was a Chinese international student at a UK university, who was interested in but new to the field of academic research. In my second year of PhD, I collaborated with two senior academics (one of which was my supervisor) in being the lead author writing for a journal article that was directly informed by the literature engagement of my PhD research. The supervision relationship had shaped our collaboration which was also a mentoring process for me to develop a first-time understanding of what might be expected for publishing in a largely UK-based, English-medium and international journal. I was the first author and also a junior researcher working with established scholars. This meant that I had an autonomous yet nurturing space of driving and shaping the article as well as being supported and guided by the other mentor-authors in the thinking and writing process. This collaboration process was an initial, significant learning journey for me. It opened my door to the world of academic writing for publication as a researcher transitioning from academic writing for assessment as a student. This first publication experience was the beginning of my endeavour for developing researcherhood through publication.

The publication was related to an ethical engagement with an interdisciplinary, intercultural and multilingual concept: 'mindfulness' in English, or '念' (nian) in Chinese (Huang, Fay, & White, 2017). With my supervisor's guidance, we first presented our joint thinking around the intercultural ethics of working with such a concept in an international conference (Huang, Fay, & White, 2015). Following the conference, we then developed the paper for the conference special issue. I learnt that this route from conferences to their special issues could usually provide an access for publication. I also used this route for publication a few times after my PhD (e.g., Huang, 2020, 2021a, 2023).

Through the first publication, I recognised a few key values, such as criticality, ethics, political literacy, and activism, that might be key to the academic community in the UK higher education (HE). This reflection on the implicit marker of difference enabled my transitioning from an 'outsider' to becoming part of the academic field and community in the UK HE. My researcherhood was also influenced by the value of critical intercultural ethics, which started to develop from the first publication. For instance, I intentionally embraced my access to Chinese language sources and the opportunities for researching multilingually (Andrews & Fay, 2020; Andrews, Fay, Huang, & White, 2023; Andrews, Fay, & White, 2018a, 2018b; Andrews, Holmes, Fay, & Dawson, 2020; Fay, Andrews, Huang, & White, 2021, 2023; Holmes, Fay, Andrews, & Attia, 2013, 2016) and sought to challenge the power hierarchies of different sources and ways of knowing in various contexts. My researcherhood synthesises the socio-cultural, linguistic, conceptual, and methodological distinctiveness of my identity and voices as a researcher – as well as the development of professional belonging and dialogues with peer researchers in the intercultural field. I also realised that my publications may provide solidarity with peer researchers who were from similar backgrounds working internationally, probably struggling publishing ideas originated from other languages in English-medium academic journals.

PUBLISHING FROM THE PHD

I used the original contributions of my thesis to develop various publications after the PhD. These involved work along the lines of concepts such as 'intercultural personhood' (Huang, 2021a) and 'intercultural mindfulness' (Huang, 2023), creative arts methods such as 'blind-portrait' (Huang, 2022a), imagination and painting (Huang, 2021b), 'multi-slicing semiotic analysis' (MSA) (Huang, 2017) and critical approaches such as non-essentialism, intercultural ethics and epistemic justice (Huang, 2022b). Within the tight timeline of a PhD study, I was not able to publish on all of these aspects. After the PhD study, however, I worked as an academic in the same department. Now, I had the time and space to transform the above aspects of my thesis into publications. This process (of transforming knowledge and skills from the PhD thesis to peer-reviewed journal articles) had also mirrored my transformation from a PhD student to an early career academic at the time – another key stage of developing my researcherhood and professional belonging.

I recognised that publishing from the PhD requires a clear purpose for each article, a purpose that is different from the purpose of a PhD thesis. In other words, whereas those aspects of the thesis had served the purpose of the PhD research questions, what would be the central purpose or question for each new article? This question guided me to develop six articles with different focuses from my PhD thesis. By transforming the thesis into articles, I further articulated and developed my researcherhood in various areas. For instance, in one article, I reflected on my being and becoming of an artist–researcher (or 'artist–researcherhood') and how it had informed my design and use of blind portrait as a creative art method (see section 'Artist–researcher' in Huang, 2022a).

PUBLISHING BEYOND THE PHD

Beyond publishing from the PhD thesis, my endeavour of publication was mainly informed by (a) applying/extending my PhD into wider contexts/projects and/or (b) developing new projects with colleagues from the teaching and learning practice. For instance, following my work with my supervisor on mindfulness, epistemic justice and intercultural ethics, I was later involved in other related publications (such as Andrews, Fay, Huang, & White, 2023; De Stefani, Fay, & Huang, 2024; Fay, Andrews, Huang, & White, 2021, 2023) from my supervisor's networks. I also developed articles with colleagues about our practices of teaching, learning and student experience, such as internationalising reference lists in students' assignments (Lim & Huang, 2022), reconceptualising an 'international' subject (Huang, Cockayne, & Mittelmeier, 2024) and student belonging and photography (Huang & Cockayne, 2023). These articles were part of the outcomes from various scholarship projects that I undertook during my academic teaching roles at the university.

The process of developing the above publications provided me with opportunities to further develop my researcherhood as part of the academic community in the university and wider networks. I was able to synthesise the distinctiveness of my research interests in creative arts methods and critical intercultural education with peer researchers' endeavours in the wider fields such as education internationalisation, music education and teacher education. This synthesis process highlights dialogues, cross-fertilisations, academic solidarity (Bieliauskaitė, 2021) within the communities of the university, HE and the relevant research fields. Such a process provided me with a rich ground and a sense of responsibility for developing my professional belonging through publication.

CONCLUDING REFLECTIONS

In this narrative, I have reflected on my development of researcherhood and professional belonging from my PhD study to an early career stage. My development of the eclectic academic profile was not so much from a conscious strategic plan but driven by my research interests from my PhD and later my teaching and learning practices. A thread through these was a passion for conceptual and methodological innovations and critical intercultural ethics in educational research. As outlined above, my journey had moved from co-authoring to a string of single-authored publications and back to co-authoring. After my first co-authoring experience for publication, I was eager to 'test-drive' my publication skills in order to become an independent researcher/author for publication. I produced a few publications as a single author, which were also mainly from my own PhD study. After that, my co-authored publications were informed by my collaborative practices with colleagues and by an intention of appreciating the joy and learning through joint publication processes. Part of that joy is to feel connected and contributed as an academic to a community and thereby to develop a sense of researcherhood and professional belonging.

My reflections are situated in the contexts of my individual experience but may offer ideas resonating with similar experiences or circumstances of fellow doctoral students and early career academics. Writing the chapter itself is also a reflective process for me to make sense of my researcherhood and professional belonging. My individual stories and experiences can hopefully contribute to enriching the collective resources and dialogues about the trajectory from doctoral student to published author in the wider community, including PhD alumni and beyond.

REFERENCES

Andrews, J., & Fay, R. (2020). Valuing a translingual mindset in researcher education in Anglophone higher education settings: Supervision perspectives. *Language, Culture and Curriculum*, *33*(2), 188–202.

Andrews, J., Fay, R., Huang, Z. M., & White, R. G. (2023). From translanguaging to transknowledging: Exploring new epistemological and linguistic approaches in higher education research. In J. Huisman & M. Tight (Eds.), *Theory and method in higher education research* (pp. 137–151). Emerald Publishing Limited.

Andrews, J., Fay, R., & White, R. G. (2018a). From linguistic preparation to developing a translingual orientation – Possible implications of plurilingualism for researcher education. In J. Choi & S. Ollerhead (Eds.), *Plurilingualism in learning and teaching: complexities across contexts* (pp. 220–233). Routledge.

Andrews, J., Fay, R., & White, R. G. (2018b). What shapes everyday translanguaging? Insights from a global mental health research project in Northern Uganda. In G. Mazzaferro (Ed.), *Translanguaging in everyday practice* (pp. 257–273). Springer.

Andrews, J., Holmes, P., Fay, R., & Dawson, S. (2020). Researching multilingually in applied linguistics. In H. Rose & J. McKinley (Eds.), *Routledge handbook of research methods in applied linguistics* (pp. 76–86). Routledge.

Barnard, H. A. (2019). Developing researcherhood: Identity tensions and identity work of women academics reflecting on their researcher identity. *Qualitative Social Research*, *20*(3). https://doi.org/10.17169/fqs-20.3.3238

Bieliauskaitė, J. (2021). Solidarity in academia and its relationship to academic integrity. *Journal of Academic Ethics*, *19*(3), 309–322.

De Stefani, M., Fay, R., & Huang, Z. M. (2024). English for research purposes and linguistic diversity: Researcher reflexivity and social justice. In P. Breen & M. le Roux (Eds.), *Social justice in EAP and ELT contexts: Global higher education perspectives* (pp. 197–210). Bloomsbury.

Fay, R., Andrews, J., Huang, Z. M., & White, R. G. (2021). Bringing the critical into doctoral supervision: What can we learn from debates about epistemic justice and the languaging of research? *Journal of Praxis in Higher Education*, *3*(2), 104–127. https://doi.org/10.47989/kpdc109

Fay, R., Andrews, J., Huang, Z. M., & White, R. G. (2023). Linguistic diversity in research with any by international students: Considerations for research design and practice. In J. Mittelmeier, S. Lomer, & K. Unkule (Eds.), *Researching with international students: Critical and methodological considerations* (pp. 255–265). Routledge.

Holmes, P., Fay, R., Andrews, J., & Attia, M. (2013). Researching multilingually: New theoretical and methodological directions. *International Journal of Applied Linguistics*, *23*(3), 285–299.

Holmes, P., Fay, R., Andrews, J., & Attia, M. (2016). How to research multilingually: Possibilities and complexities. In Z. Hua (Ed.), *Research methods in intercultural communication: A practical Guide* (pp. 88–102). Wiley.

Huang, Z. M. (2017). Multislicing semiotic analysis (MSA): Engaging with the meanings of creative-visual-arts data. In P. Burnard, V. Ross, T. Dragovic, H. Minors, K. Powell, & L. Mackinlay (Eds.), *Building intercultural and interdisciplinary bridges: Where theory meets research and practice* (pp. 104–112). BIBACC Publishing.

Huang, Z. M. (2019). *Mindfulness and intercultural personhood: Understanding students' intercultural experience at a culturally-diverse UK university*. PhD Thesis. The University of Manchester.

Huang, Z. M. (2020). Learning from the 'right' ground of mindfulness: Some insights for the 'good' interculturalist. *Language and Intercultural Communication*, *20*(1), 1–12. https://doi.org/10.1080/14708477.2019.1672711

Huang, Z. M. (2021a). Intercultural personhood: A non-essentialist conception of individuals for intercultural research. *Language and Intercultural Communication*, *21*(1), 83–101. https://doi.org/10.1080/14708477.2020.1833898

Huang, Z. M. (2021b). Exploring imagination as a methodological source of knowledge: Painting students' intercultural experience at a UK university. *International Journal of Research & Method in Education*, *44*(4), 366–378. https://doi.org/10.1080/1743727X.2020.1796958

Huang, Z. M. (2022a). 'Blind'-portrait: Using arts methods to de-essentialise intercultural, educational research. *Language and Intercultural Communication*, 22(2), 176–190. https://doi.org/10.1080/14708477.2022.2041653

Huang, Z. M. (2022b). A critical understanding of students' intercultural experience in internationalised HE: Non-essentialism and epistemic justice. *Intercultural Education*, 33(3), 247–263. https://doi.org/10.1080/14675986.2022.2069393

Huang, Z. M. (2023). Intercultural mindfulness: Artistic meaning-making about students' intercultural experience at a UK university. *Language and Intercultural Communication*, 23(1), 36–52. https://doi.org/10.1080/14708477.2022.2162064

Huang, Z. M., & Cockayne, H. (2023). Searching for belonging: Learning from students' photographs about their higher education experiences. *London Review of Education*, 21(1), 27.

Huang, Z. M., Cockayne, H., & Mittelmeier, J. (2024). Towards diverse, critical understandings of "international" for higher education. *Equality, Diversity and Inclusion*. https://doi.org/10.1108/EDI-08-2023-0277

Huang, Z. M., Fay, R., & White, R. G. (2015, November). Intercultural knowledge-work and the transcultural development of ideas: 念(niàn)/mindfulness, intercultural communication, and psychotherapy. Paper presented at *The Fifteenth IALIC Conference*, Peking University, China, November 27, 2015.

Huang, Z. M., Fay, R., & White, R. G. (2017). 念(niàn)/Mindfulness and the ethics of intercultural knowledge-work. *Language and Intercultural Communication*, *17*(1), 45–57. https://doi.org/10.1080/14708477.2017.1261672

Lim, M. A., & Huang, Z. M. (2022). An analysis of Chinese students' use of 'Chinese' essay references: Another role for international students in the internationalisation of the curriculum. *Learning and Teaching: International Journal of Higher Education*, *15*(2), 29–52. https://doi.org/10.3167/latiss.2022.150203

12

BUILDING YOUR 'LOOP' IN NAVIGATING AN ACADEMIC COMMUNITY

RUI HE

The University of Manchester, UK

> Rui He is currently a Lecturer in Education at The University of Manchester. She joined Lantern quite recently having undertaken her postgraduate studies elsewhere in the United Kingdom. Her PhD in Education (He, 2021a) focused on the acculturation experiences of foreign language learners in Chinese and British study abroad programmes. Before graduation, she collaboratively published an article (Cai et al., 2019) and a chapter (Elliot, He & Dangeni, 2019) both focused on aspects of doctoral study rather than on her own particular area of doctoral research. Many of her works since graduation are similarly collaborative. In this narrative, she asks some important questions including: 'What are the knowledge and skills needed to
>
> (*Continued*)

> (*Continued*)
>
> navigate the rules of the publishing game in different institutions and broadly this academic community?' In it, she recognises that navigating the academic community is not just about publishing itself but also about how to manage a healthy balance between herself and academia. Her LOOP framework captures her insights into this managing this challenge.

RESEARCHING AND EXPERIENCING INTERCULTURALITY

As an intercultural researcher and a sojourner (i.e., I did my doctoral degree and now working as an early career researcher [ECR] in the United Kingdom), I believe that what makes intercultural studies fascinating is the intricacies involved in balancing the brightness and darkness in an overseas/intercultural journey. Physically moving to the United Kingdom meant I would lose familiar 'sources of support' (Elliot, Reid, & Baumfield, 2016, p. 2214), such as my family and friends, my favourite local restaurant!. It was as if I was turning back into a 3-month-old and trying to learn how to talk, think, behave or do things (maybe even how to eat, given that it took my hot food-favoured stomach several years to welcome cold dishes such as sandwiches and salads!) in an environment with great cultural differences from my home one.

However, this navigation also provided a meaningful learning opportunity for me to revisit and scrutinise practices from different cultures (Elliot et al., 2016). Eventually, I managed to rebuild new developmental ecological systems (Bronfenbrenner & Morris, 2006; He, 2021a, b) for my sojourn in the United Kingdom. For example, I found a replacement of my favourite local restaurant at home: a café near my student accommodation when I was doing my doctoral study, I almost went there every day, either for grabbing a coffee or doing some work. It, then, became an important source of support, familiarity and comfort to me. Whenever I returned from other cities or countries, it would be the first place I would go to.

Interestingly, such navigation between cultures and ecological systems in my own sojourn also inspired and shaped my academic thinking and identity, leading to my strong research interest in exploring how people better rebuild their supportive systems for development, in whichever environment or scenarios they will be. I realise that an individual's agency plays a crucial role in exploring surroundings and locating and managing resources for development (He, 2021a), and more importantly, many of such navigations begin with trivial, commonplace things, which people tend to overlook in daily life. An interesting example of this thinking forms part of my recent co-authored publication (He, Köksal, Cockayne, & Elliot, 2024) about food and international students' acculturation experiences.

As an ECR, such navigation happened in my workplace – academic community – as well. Starting as an international doctoral student from a different country and educational/professional system, it was not surprising that it took me substantial amount of time and effort to navigate the new community and its 'rules of the game,' e.g., different academic standards, institutional policies and expectations, to manage work relationships and develop researcher independence and identity, and publications – all essential components in this community. Writing academically in a foreign language is already challenging, let alone the overwhelming navigations of the new publishing process and rules in a new and unfamiliar community.

What are the knowledge and skills needed to navigate the rules of the publishing game in different institutions and broadly this academic community? Where can I find the sources of support? There were so many questions for me, not only when I was a doctoral student but also, maybe even more confusing, when I am now an ECR. Some institutions might offer training courses on academic writing or writing for publications for doctoral students, but many universities may take for granted that their new members of staff know all policies about publication at the particular institution, which is not very likely to be the case for many ECRs, or at least not for me.

After getting lost for weeks, I realised that navigating the academic community was indeed an overwhelming challenge, but it is not just about publishing itself, it is more about how I can manage a healthy balance between me and the academia. It could also be a great opportunity to rebuild my supportive ecological systems for my professional development, like how I navigated and survived in the foreign country. Then I started my experiment on the LOOP theory I proposed (inspired by my own efforts in finding the café as a replacement for my favourite restaurant at home).[1]

LOOP: LINKING

Taking publication as an example, I began my navigation in this academic publishing game with *linking* the 'sources of support' I need for getting one publication done successfully.

---

[1] The arguments raised here originated from the author's invited talk at University of Glasgow April Career Lunch on April 5, 2022.

I needed to explore what is required, by whom and when, what resources are available and how I can access them. Technically, it involves the knowledge and skills of academic writing in a foreign language, publishing procedures and requirements in the UK academia, the expectations and policies at my institution. Therefore, I tried to find out what training resources, documents such as policies and handbooks are available within and beyond my institution.

However, as I mentioned earlier, many navigations involve, or even begin with, commonplace things people tend to overlook in daily life. While collecting these resources, I felt that I may need something else: for example, I need a comfortable place for writing (which is very important to me), someone as a critical friend to discuss my arguments and flow of writing, etc. Involving my parents at home as critical friends was another really interesting experiment I had at this step even though they knew little about my research work (He, 2021b). Being physically distant from home is challenging, and I have always tried to find a way to continue the connections with my parents who are one of the strongest, most familiar sources of support to me. Therefore, sometimes I would ask them to read my writing or explain a challenging idea to them and ask them to raise any questions whenever they have. Guess what: by doing this, you will get the most difficult reviewers in the world! But thanks to my parents, they raised quite a lot of unanticipated questions at surprising places in the manuscript (e.g., *you were discussing A and why did you jump to B now without finishing the discussion on A?*). These questions were completely out of my expectations but genuinely helpful and made me realised how taken-for-granted I was in writing certain parts: e.g., *I thought I have finished the discussion on A and everyone knows enough about A while apparently it was not the case for different audiences/readers.*

LOOP: OPPORTUNITIES

Sometimes when mapping out the resources and trying to link the most relevant and available 'source of support' I need for a publication, some unanticipated *opportunities* came up. For instance, I planned to write a journal article when I came across a book chapter invitation which looked like a perfect home for the content I planned to write about. When I blocked some time for writing a new paper, a colleague reached out and invited me to co-author another paper. Or, sometimes, when I met a new friend who became an important 'source of support' in my new supportive ecological system abroad, I then realised the shared interest between us may lead to a potential collaboration on a publication. None of them were in the initial plan but apparently; they were great opportunities. Also, some collaboration opportunities seem to become an effective tool for dealing with my procrastination because the guilt I may have for collaborators from any delays keeps me productive!

However, many times, for various reasons, opportunities did not come up as I hoped. For example, I missed a good home for a publication (a special issue call) because the deadline had already passed when I came across the call, or I would like to learn some techniques in relation to publications, but such trainings were not available at my institution. Then, I had to change my plans until the opportunities come up.

LOOP: (AM I) OKAY?

I used to feel extremely guilty if I missed a good opportunity or could not manage to cover all the available resources I have linked (which I find to be a very naïve and impossible thought now). Such guilty brought nothing positive but bad work–life balance, personal mental and physical well-being, and not surprisingly, these elements could easily result in a vicious cycle.

Some people started worrying about publications when they started their doctoral studies, while some may start later, but it is very likely to be a constant worry in academia. Such issues, unfortunately, did not get better when I started the full-time job. Understanding and managing various responsibilities and new rules from the new role at a new institution already made my life a non-stop move in the first year, leaving little brain space for peaceful thinking and writing. Additionally, peer pressure (especially from native English-speaking peers) only adds on stress and aggravate imposter syndrome for me. In the end, it led to burnout.

I was troubled by this issue until one day – a typical guilty day – the owner at the café I often visited asked me 'are you okay?' Then I realised that I had never asked myself if I am *okay* with all these opportunities and resources: Do I really need them all? At the same time? With equal time and effort? How can I become more strategic with them? How can I be less guilty but enjoying the new community and game?

LOOP: PRIORITISE

Then, the questions above led me to the final step of my experiment: *prioritise* my time, energy and tasks based on several potential criteria:

- How relevant is it?

- How possible is it with my current schedule?

- How much would I enjoy it?

Sometimes, a tricky situation could be between a very relevant, enjoyable solo-authored work and collaborative work for just one possible timeline. Then I asked myself another question:

- What do I value most from this opportunity or resource?
- What future opportunities or plans could be available for the one I may choose or the one I may give up this time?

People in different roles, at different stages or with different goals and personalities may develop different criteria for their prioritisation, but I found these questions helpful starting points for considerations when deciding a topic for a paper, collaborators for particular topic or type of publication or timeline. Most importantly, careful considerations on these questions have greatly alleviated my guilty and imposter syndrome and supported me in developing a healthy and sustainable balance between me and the academia, as well as a comfortable academic identity and working style.

In the intercultural field, scholars argue that human development does not stop when one physically moves to a new cultural environment while, at the same time, such intensive intercultural contact and interactions orchestrate transformative changes and development on the individual sojourners (Elliot et al., 2016; He, 2021a). Navigating academic community or academic culture (or specifically publication culture) could be a good example of such transformative changes and development. The four steps discussed above (link, opportunities, (am I) okay, and prioritise) construct my proposed LOOP theory, which became a powerful principle and tool to help me navigate the academic community and manage changes and development as an ECR more comfortably and effectively.

REFERENCES

Bronfenbrenner, U., & Morris, P. (2006). The bioecological model of human development. In W. Damon & R. Lerner (Eds.), *Handbook of child psychology, Theoretical models of human development* (6th ed., Vol. 1, pp. 793–828). John Wiley.

Cai, L., Dangeni, D., Elliot, D. L., He, R., Liu, J., Makara, K. A., Pacheco, E. M., Shih, K., Wang, W., & Zhang, J. (2019). A conceptual inquiry of communities of practice as praxis in international doctoral education. *Journal for Praxis in Higher Education, 1*(1), 11–36.

Elliot, D., He, R., & Dangeni (2019). Setting and adjusting expectations of supervision. In M. Dolinger (Ed.), *Getting the most out of your doctorate: The importance of supervision, networking, and becoming a global academic* (pp. 19–34). Emerald Publishing Limited.

Elliot, D. L., Reid, K., & Baumfield, V. (2016). Beyond the amusement, puzzlement and challenges: An enquiry into international students' academic acculturation. *Studies in Higher Education, 41*(12), 2198–2217. https://doi.org/10.1080/03075079.2015.1029903

He, R. (2021a). *A 'mirror-image' investigation: Foreign language learners' acculturation experiences in Chinese and British study abroad programmes*. PhD Thesis. University of Glasgow. http://theses.gla.ac.uk/82185/

He, R. (2021b). The 'loop-building' initiative. *The Hidden Curriculum in Doctoral Education*. https://drhiddencurriculum.wordpress.com/2021/08/09/the-loop-building-initiative/

He, R., Köksal, S., Cockayne, H., & Elliot, D. L. (2024). It's more than just food: The role of food among Chinese international students' acculturation experiences in the UK and USA. Advance Access. *Food, Culture & Society*, *28*(1), 306–324.

13

HOW PRACTICE SHAPES RESEARCH AND A SENSE OF COMMUNITY IN THE FIELD OF ENGLISH FOR ACADEMIC PURPOSES

PAUL BREEN

University College London, UK

> Paul is another pioneer of the 'in context' (i.e., distance learning mode) doctoral programme at The University of Manchester. His thesis (Breen, 2015) focuses on English for Academic Purposes (EAP), an area also at the heart of his publications (e.g., Breen, 2018; Breen & le Roux, 2024). EAP is also an area which sits within many university contexts without necessarily being linked to an active area of research practice. Paul's narrative is a challenge to that situation – understanding the relationship between EAP as professional practice and research focus is central to his story.

ENGLISH FOR ACADEMIC PURPOSES: PRACTITIONERS AND RESEARCHERS

There appears to be an increasing awareness that for EAP to be treated the same as other sectors of academia, it needs to engage in the same type of activities. That is why many places such as my current workplace have been making serious efforts to acculturate EAP practitioners into the wider habitat of academic research. Partly, this has also been influenced by the success of the University College Union in arguing that all university staff must be given dedicated time for research since it is only socially just that both cultural and economic conditions foster the espoused values of institutions. Without one form of justice the other cannot exist (Gray, 2024) and the affordance of time has been critical to triggering a vibrant research culture.

In order to enact and quantify the time given to building and sustaining such a culture, my particular department within the university has created the space for a scholarly community. This space has been informally named as a 'Collegial Space' and takes the form of a weekly meeting facilitated through *Microsoft Teams* and lasting for at least an hour in each enactment. This virtual space allows for a shared review of activity, such as design and delivery of courses, alongside discussions about what types of scholarly work we are doing or want to do.

As such, it is putting into practice self-directed development as discussed in Ding and Bruce (2017, pp. 139–152) or Steve Mann's (2005) work where he speaks of teacher development being a 'bottom-up process' that values the 'insider' view (p. 105). Ultimately, the goal is to use this space as a means of fostering a culture of teaching-informed research and research-informed teaching.

That of course is a long-established feature of educational research, going right back to Kurt Lewin (1946, p. 34), who championed the benefits of 'research which will help the practitioner' up to Anne Burns (1999, p. 24) who speaks of research often being prompted by 'concrete and practical' issues of 'immediate concern' in the workplace. For a great many people within EAP, this is where the road to research begins –a place close to home. That is how it began for me, with my opening forays into the world of publishing coming about through work that I was doing around integration of technology into my practice. That would eventually become the focus of my PhD research too, where a sense of academic community was central to shaping my first academic publications.

These publishing forays were largely based around my doctoral studies (Breen, 2015), which focused on an exploration of teacher development in the particular context in which I was working. That was a study of how EAP practitioners develop in terms of both pedagogical and technological knowledge, after embarking on a series of teacher education workshops. As such, it was rooted in a study of people and practices rather than language and featured a Community of Practice (CoP) that evolved organically out of the workshops rather than being planned or cultivated, as discussed in the work of Lave and Wenger (1991) and Wenger (1998). At the same time, it was not completely organic. There were Vygotskian-based elements to the evolution of this CoP, particularly in the forms of self-regulation that teachers developed both individually and as a group.

FROM STUDYING TO BUILDING ACADEMIC COMMUNITIES

In the same way, my university's 'Collegial Space' has seen a shared set of developments taking place, where scholarly development has also been cultivated and then allowed to grow through participants' interactions with one another. Already, just over a year into the creation of this space, several small-scale research projects have taken shape, often enacted by early-career researchers not necessarily at doctoral level just yet, which of course should not disbar anyone from scholarly activity.

Generally, such projects will focus on student needs. For example, one group of colleagues has investigated the notion of 'brave spaces' as opposed to 'safe spaces' (Arao & Clemens, 2013) in the context of student engagement and well-being. Though their explorations of this phenomenon have been informal so far, there has been a knock-on effect in terms of the sharing of knowledge. As a result of being exposed to this idea within our Collegial Space, I then discussed it in my own work writing about enactments of Social Justice in EAP and ELT contexts (Breen & le Roux, 2024). Subsequently, these ideas have bled out into the wider domain and others who are writing about Social Justice have now also incorporated 'brave spaces' into their language and writing.

However, the seeds that have been cultivated through our Collegial Space are not simply theoretical. There have also been practical projects initiated, instigated and enacted, with the student voice and the student experience again at the heart of these. Most recently, some of these projects have entailed research into aspects of Generative AI, demonstrating the cutting-edge, interdisciplinary nature of Academic English.

One such instance of collegial teamworking entailed an exploration into *Using AI tools for the reading-into-writing process* (UCL, 2023), where three students were invited to reflect on writing an assignment with the assistance of AI tools, as part of a teacher/student co-creator project. Three members of our team, including the Head of the Centre, participated in this study of if and how students used the new technologies at their disposal in the digital age and how they felt that this impacted on their learning and assessment experiences at the university as a whole. The findings that emerged through this subsequently had both theoretical and practical impact within the wider university, bringing EAP practitioners out of the margins and not just into the mainstream but becoming active players in shaping practices and policies of the wider university. In practice, this meant the development of recommendations 'to facilitate discussions around appropriate use of AI tools in the reading-into-writing process' (UCL, 2023).

Thanks to this project, the people involved produced a publication in the form of a blog post and as such offered something tangible through scholarly activity. The publication of research does not have to be limited to such things as journal articles. Nowadays, there are multiple outlets and purposes of academic publishing. The act of writing anything also provides not just professional but personal benefit, it appears. Getting published is a vital part of our personal development and acculturation into the academic community, particularly for those deemed early-career researchers.

WRITING IN AN ACADEMIC COMMUNITY

Whether for immediate career benefit or not, getting published can provide a stimulus for other forms of development that will enrich the new researcher's participation in the educational ecosystem. The first way in which it does this is to give confidence to novice researchers and to assist in developing their own academic voices. Furthermore, by concentrating on the de facto home turf of student writing practices, these colleagues have helped take away some of the mystique of publication. Some novice researchers might be intimidated by the language around much of the present EAP research culture, which seems to prioritise theoretical aspects of language above the practical aspects of what teachers do on a daily basis (teaching).

Most of our daily practices are shaped by pedagogy, whether in areas of teaching, materials design, technological aspects, the student experience or countless other instances of things to do with language but not explicitly language alone, which is what the bulk of EAP publishing presently concentrates on. By somehow managing to give greater credence to the importance of these other practical aspects, more people within EAP might feel increased confidence about the possibility of publishing. It might also help us as a discipline because in my opinion there is a need to make EAP more practical and more socially just, particularly in light of recent developments around Generative AI. This will undoubtably change the future of language teaching, and these are the sorts of issues that EAP scholarship should be engaging with rather than to some extent shunning.

To begin with, in the case of EAP, we need to make publishing opportunities feel more accessible. To do that, there probably should be more of an emphasis on researching and writing about the things that the majority of us are doing on a daily basis. Until we accept teaching itself as a valuable part of what we do and who we are, we are not just failing to realise our potential in higher education, but we are also failing to recognise our own replication of hierarchical ideologies endemic to the wider academy.

Though community plays a major part in the activity system of EAP, for many practitioners there is a sense of working in their own islands. Yet that can be a strength rather than a weakness. Our islands of practice within the EAP domain are context-rich and shaped by a sense of community, within which we need to work together to develop as practitioners whose output is not solely defined by scholarly research, but by scholarship-informed teaching that leads to other forms of more practice-based output. Pedagogy, especially at a time of such rapid technological development, is our greatest strength and the core of our knowledge base.

This, to my mind, is an area in which we need to be creating more opportunities for publication. Through initiatives such as that which we have developed at UCL, there is an opportunity for people to develop and thrive, making practical contributions to the activity systems within which they work. We need to be a vital part of higher education's ecosystem, not an island in the margins, and scholarly activity is the best way to bring us into the mainstream.

However, it is important to remember that all of this is not a single-shot process. There is a need for constant review and sharing of practice, reflecting on developments and acting upon that reflection, which has also been a key feature of the context in which I work. That, aptly, is an Academic Communication Centre and has taught me a great deal about communicating our research within a team.

REFERENCES

Arao, B., & Clemens, K. (2013). From safe spaces to brave spaces: A new way to frame dialogue around diversity and social justice. In L. Landreman (Ed.), *The art of effective facilitation: Reflections from social justice educators* (pp. 135–150). Stylus Publishing.

Breen, P. (2015). *Teachers in transition: developing actions, knowledge and practice in the EAP classroom*. PhD Thesis. The University of Manchester.

Breen, P. (2018). *Developing educators for the digital age: A framework for capturing knowledge in action.* University of Westminster Press.

Breen, P., & le Roux, M. (Eds.). (2024). *Social justice in EAP and ELT contexts.* Bloomsbury.

Burns, A. (1999). *Collaborative action research for English language teachers.* Cambridge University Press.

Ding, A., & Bruce, I. (2017). *The English for academic purposes practitioner: Operating on the edge of academia.* Springer.

Gray, J. (2024). Foreword. In P. Breen & M. Le Roux (Eds.), *Social justice in EAP and ELT contexts* (pp. xvii–xxi). Bloomsbury.

Lave, J., & Wenger, E. (1991). *Situated learning: Legitimate peripheral participation.* Cambridge University Press.

Lewin, K. (1946). Action research and minority problems. *Journal of Social Issues*, 2(4), 34–46.

Mann, S. J. (2005). The language teacher's development. *Language Teaching*, 38(3), 103–118.

UCL Teaching and Learning Blog. (2023, October 19). Using AI tools for the reading-into-writing process. *Digital Education Case Studies Blog.* https://www.ucl.ac.uk/teaching-learning/case-studies/2023/oct/using-ai-tools-reading-writing-process

Wenger, E. (1998). *Communities of practice: Learning, meaning, and identity.* Cambridge University Press.

COMMENTARY TO PART D

RICHARD FAY[a] AND ACHILLEAS KOSTOULAS[b]

[a]The University of Manchester, UK
[b]University of Thessaly, Greece

The contributions that make up Part D include descriptions of communities of practice involved in social writing practices (see Andrews, Chapter 2, this volume), more abstract narrations of developing professional belonging and discussions about how to introduce agency in engaging with the affordances that academic communities present.

One theme that these accounts highlight is the challenges ECRs face in positioning themselves within the ideas, practices, expectations and discourses that are typical of international academia, a move, which for Min and Rui (and countless other academics in an increasingly mobile academic world) was complicated by physical relocation and acculturation into a new community. This process adds a new dimension to the process of intentional becoming (Stelma & Kostoulas, 2021) that was discussed in Part A: namely identifying affordances, such as collaboration opportunities, peer support groups and more, acting on them (or perhaps choosing not to do so) and reshaping oneself and the community through such action.

What Min, Rui, and Paul's contributions illustrate is how academic publishing, though intrinsically challenging, seems to have acted as a driver for intentional becoming. Min's publishing trajectory began with co-authored papers, which involved redefining her role as an outsider to UK academia, as a woman in a system that is still informed by patriarchal norms and as a junior academic working with more established collaborators. This eventually gave her the confidence to produce a string of single-authored publications, and approach collaborative projects from a more empowered perspective. Similarly, Rui's narrative shows how ECRs can shape this process in an intentional way, by purposefully navigating affordances and creating new ones that are consistent with her motivations and aspirations. Lastly, Paul's contribution highlights how a writing community of practice can provide a safe structured space for ECRs to explore and create affordances for their development.

Academic becoming, then, is not a process of assimilation into academia. What the three narratives show is that communities of practice can create an affordance-rich environment for developing through publication and that ECRs can assume a more agentic role in the process.

REFERENCE

Stelma, J., & Kostoulas, A. (2021). *The intentional dynamics of TESOL*. De Gruyter Mouton.

Part E

ENGAGING WITH PUBLISHERS

14

DILEMMAS AND CHALLENGES IN PUBLICATION AND REVISION OF RESEARCH ARTICLES AS AN EARLY CAREER RESEARCHER

DUYGU CANDARLI

University of Southampton, UK

Duygu is currently a Lecturer in TESOL at the University of Southampton. She completed her doctoral studies at The University of Manchester, and she has published in international journals such as *Corpora* (Candari & Jones, 2019), the *Journal of English for Academic Purposes* (Candarli, Bayyurt, & Martı, 2015), and *Language Learning Journal* (Candarli, 2020), and *Reading and Writing* (Candarli, 2021). Her research specialisation lies in second language writing and broadly corpus linguistics.

In her narrative, writing purposefully in more conversational style than she normally uses for academic writing, she reflects on some dilemmas and challenges she has experienced as an ECR whilst submitting
(Continued)

> (*Continued*)
>
> research articles, revising and finally seeing them published. She feels that the emotional aspects of reviewer feedback, whilst discipline-specific, may resonate with ECR experiences in other disciplines (e.g., applied linguistics).

DILEMMA: TO COMPARE OR NOT TO COMPARE AND WHAT TO COMPARE

Research on second language writing (L2 or Lx writing) is inherently comparative, especially when we use corpus linguistics techniques (see Hyland, 2016). An important consideration when we examine L2 writing is whether we compare it with first language writing (L1 writing) or another reference corpus that can be regarded as the benchmark. More importantly, when we compare L2 writing with L1 writing, the important question remains as to how L1 writing should be conceptualised. Is it a reference corpus (benchmark) or an L1 variety of English? This is still a contentious issue not only in L2 writing but also in other subfields of applied linguistics (see De Houwer, 2023; Dewaele, Bak, & Ortega, 2021). I argue for a more plausible alternative to the dilemma of L1 versus L2 writing, which is a longitudinal comparison of L2 writing in its own right to track changes and developments of the same students over time.

In a study derived from my PhD, I conducted a longitudinal investigation of multi-word constructions (e.g., 'on the other hand') in L2 writing (Candarli, 2021). However, I have experienced the abovementioned dilemmas since I started researching L2 writing for my MA thesis. In my MA thesis, I compared metadiscourse features between L1 and L2 novice writers of English. Although we argued in our paper (Candarli, Bayyurt, & Marti, 2015) that both groups were novices who were learning to write academic essays partly due to the similarities that we found in the use of metadiscourse features, especially boosters, the monolingual L1 writing was used as the reference corpus without considering writing quality or any proxies of writing quality, such as grades. Later on, influential papers advocating for 'equitable multilingualism' in second language acquisition and beyond (e.g., Douglas Fir Group, 2016; Ortega, 2019) convinced me that comparing L2 writing with monolingual L1 writing as the reference corpus is neither fair nor illuminating without considering contextual factors in depth. This is not to say that I am now against the comparison of L1 versus L2 writing; however, I am convinced that monolingual L1 writing may not be the golden standard for L2 writers who are bilingual or multilingual.

Given that L1 writing is heterogenous and changes across time (see Staples, Egbert, Biber, & Gray, 2016), research on writing across different L1 groups, while taking into account other factors, such as genre and writing quality, is informative to offer implications for teaching and assessment in educational contexts (see Candarli, 2022a). In such cases, it is more equitable to conceptualise L1 writing as a variety of L1 English rather than the norm or benchmark for L2 writers. It is useful to note that although there is now a considerable body of research that advocates for changes in our research practices (e.g., Douglas Fir Group, 2016; Ortega, 2019), the effect of this advocacy on research practices has been slow. In the revision process of a publication, you may find yourself reverting back to comparing L1 writing (as the reference corpus) versus L2 writing to publish the study.

DILEMMA: TO PUBLISH JOURNAL ARTICLES OR A MONOGRAPH OR BOTH AFTER MY PHD

The second dilemma that I faced after finishing my PhD was whether to publish journal articles or a monograph. If you research on this issue, there are different suggestions in the literature on applied linguistics (see Paltridge, 2016). I published two journal articles and one book chapter out of my PhD study (see Candarli, 2020, 2021, 2022b). These publications required substantial reworking of my PhD, new data analyses and considerable rewriting. The same applies to publishing a book (see Paltridge, 2016 for an example). Upon reflection now, I could have also published a monograph after publishing the journal articles and a book chapter. My external examiner suggested that I publish a monograph so that I could present my arguments and contributions in a more coherent manner in a mixed-methods study that involved both corpus linguistics techniques and interviews. I could have listened to her advice and also published a monograph after journal articles.

The other dilemma is how many publications we could write out of our PhD study without 'salami slicing', which refers to 'the practice of splitting a single academic study, which could easily be published as a single body of work, into multiple publications or "slices" that while differing little, can be spread across multiple journals to inflate the author's publication record and rank' (Adams, 2022, p. 6). Salami slicing is a contentious phenomenon that academics may not reach a consensus on. If you have a range of data types (qualitative and quantitative data) from your PhD, it is ethical to publish the results derived from them separately in different journal articles as long as the sections of research articles differ from each other substantially. According to Adams (2022), it is also ethical to publish papers on the same dataset as long as you use different theoretical or methodological frameworks to analyse the same data differently in more than one publication. It is important to raise awareness of the definition of salami slicing early on to plan publications out of PhD.

When I reflect on my post-PhD publications now, I would change my approach. I would have not moved on from my PhD topic so quickly, suggesting that I would have published one or two more research articles out of my PhD after analysing data with a different method without salami slicing. I researched two different types of multi-word constructions identified by two different methods in my PhD, but I only published data on one type, and the other type remained unpublished. When one does not publish articles out of their PhD study quickly, there will be similar publications especially when the research topic is timely. In this situation, the novelty or originality of the PhD study would fade away. Alternatively, I would have worked on a monograph after publishing research articles. At that time, I was concerned about salami slicing. However, I could have brought different analytical or theoretical lenses to my PhD and reworked on it substantially to publish a monograph. Some may argue that research articles are more important than monographs/books. However, I believe it is valuable to have a monograph on your CV if you are in social sciences or humanities disciplines. I published a co-authored monograph later on, but I did not have a monograph out of my PhD study.

CHALLENGE: THE EMOTIONAL SIDE OF PEER REVIEWERS' FEEDBACK WHEN YOU ARE AN ECR

Peer feedback in journals serves as a gatekeeping mechanism to ensure the quality of the submissions and can substantially improve the quality of manuscripts before publication. There is much written on how we address reviewers' comments when we revise and resubmit our manuscripts to the journals (e.g., Noble, 2017). However, there is much less attention to the emotional side of peer reviewers' feedback after you get your first few comments from the referees (see Jiang, 2021 for reactions to peer feedback). For instance, Jiang (2021, p. 6086) notes that 'authors may appreciate the constructive feedback in reviewers' comments while feeling sad at the rejection outcome and upset at the total amount of time spent on manuscript handling.'

When I was a fresh PhD graduate, I remember how daunting it was to read many pages of feedback (or critique of my work) and how challenging it was to separate your work from your own identity. One of my earlier responses was to read feedback multiple times on the same day I received it, which caused me to become demoralised and demotivated about the paper. As a newly minted PhD graduate, it is hard to accept that the work that you have been doing for years could be subject to pages of critique and requests for revisions.

Later on, I changed my approach. I now have a quick look at reviewers' reports when I first receive them, leave them in a separate folder on my laptop for a couple of days and return to comments with a fresh pair of eyes. In this way, I can approach the reviewers' feedback and their requests for revisions more objectively. The other reason behind this is that I now better understand the increasing demands on our time as academics who voluntarily review papers mostly in their 'own' time in a context where 'research time' is increasingly a privilege. For example, rather than thinking about why the referee asks me to make an argument or review an approach when it is already on the paper or getting frustrated about feedback, my first thinking is that maybe it is not clear to the referee; hence, it needs to be revised or foregrounded. Having said that, I sometimes read screenshots of reviewers' comments on X (formerly Twitter) that are personal assumptions or comments about the authors rather than the work itself. There is no excuse for such personal attacks, and these should be filtered out by the journal editors and not passed to the authors.

To sum up, most ECRs or academics experience these or similar dilemmas and challenges. It is normal to experience and talk about them. I aimed to normalise these by being reflective and open about my own dilemmas and challenges. It is my hope that these will be insightful for PhD researchers and ECRs.

REFERENCES

Adams, N. N. (2022). Salami slicing: Clarifying common misconceptions for social science early-career researchers. *SN Social Sciences*, *2*(7), 88. https://doi.org/10.1007/s43545-022-00389-6

Candarli, D. (2020). Changes in L2 writers' self-reported metalinguistic knowledge of lexical phrases over one academic year. *The Language Learning Journal*, *48*(6), 768–784. https://doi.org/10.1080/09571736.2018.1520914

Candarli, D. (2021). A longitudinal study of multi-word constructions in L2 academic writing: The effects of frequency and dispersion. *Reading and Writing*, *34*(5), 1191–1223. https://doi.org/10.1007/s11145-020-10108-3

Candarli, D. (2022a). Linguistic characteristics of online academic forum posts across subregisters, L1 backgrounds, and grades. *Lingua*, *267*, 103190. https://doi.org/10.1016/j.lingua.2021.103190

Candarli, D. (2022b). Combining corpus-based methods with interviews in applied linguistics research. In K. Dikilitas & K. M. Reynolds (Eds.), *Research methods in language teaching and learning: A practical guide* (pp. 166–181). Wiley-Blackwell.

Candarli, D., Bayyurt, Y., & Martı, L. (2015). Authorial presence in L1 and L2 novice academic writing: Cross-linguistic and cross-cultural perspectives. *Journal of English for Academic Purposes*, *20*, 192–202. https://doi.org/10.1016/j.jeap.2015.10.001

Candarli, D., & Jones, S. (2019). Paradigmatic influences on lexical bundles in research articles in the discipline of education. *Corpora*, *14*(2), 237–263.

De Houwer, A. (2023). The danger of bilingual–monolingual comparisons in applied psycholinguistic research. *Applied Psycholinguistics*, *44*(3), 343–357. https://doi.org/10.1017/S014271642200042X

Dewaele, J. M., Bak, T. H., & Ortega, L. (2021). Why the mythical "native speaker" has mud on its face. In N. Slavkov, S. Melo-Pfeifer, & N. Kerschhofer-Puhalo (Eds.), *The changing face of the "native speaker": Perspectives from multilingualism and globalization* (pp. 25–45). De Gruyter. https://doi.org/10.1515/9781501512353-002

Douglas Fir Group. (2016). A transdisciplinary framework for SLA in a multilingual world. *The Modern Language Journal*, *100*(S1), 19–47. https://doi.org/10.1111/modl.12301

Hyland, K. (2016). Methods and methodologies in second language writing research. *System*, *59*, 116–125. https://doi.org/10.1016/j.system.2016.05.002

Jiang, S. (2021). Understanding authors' psychological reactions to peer reviews: A text mining approach. *Scientometrics*, *126*(7), 6085–6103. https://doi.org/10.1007/s11192-021-04032-8

Noble, W. S. (2017). Ten simple rules for writing a response to reviewers. *PLoS Computational Biology*, *13*(10), e1005730. https://doi.org/10.1371/journal.pcbi.1005730

Ortega, L. (2019). SLA and the study of equitable multilingualism. *The Modern Language Journal*, *103*, 23–38. https://doi.org/10.1111/modl.12525

Paltridge, B. (2016). Publishing from a dissertation: A book or articles? In J. McKinley & H. Rose (Eds.), *Doing research in applied linguistics* (pp. 244–252). Routledge.

Staples, S., Egbert, J., Biber, D., & Gray, B. (2016). Academic writing development at the university level: Phrasal and clausal complexity across level of study, discipline, and genre. *Written Communication*, *33*(2), 149–183. https://doi.org/10.1177/0741088316631527

15

SEEKING CONSTRUCTIVE REJECTIONS: A REFLECTION ON MY PUBLICATION STRATEGIES DURING THE PHD

FELIX KWIHANGANA

The University of Manchester, UK

> Felix is another example of a teacher who came to Manchester for his MA studies and then progressed to doctoral studies (Kwihangana, 2021). Like many doctoral students, he accepted without much questioning the 'publish or perish' mantra as key to his academic future, and his narrative presents some of the hurdles he faced as he sought to achieve this published status, not least the certainty he had that his initial submissions would be rejected and that he would need to be able to learn from the feedback accompanying these rejections. Being able to learn from engagement with editors and reviewers is one key insight he has to offer; the other is to avoid the tunnel vision that can result from the 'publish or perish' mantra.

WRITING TO BECOME AN ACADEMIC

At the start of my PhD, I had decided that I wanted to become an academic. Ironically, despite having been encouraged throughout my MA training to consider disseminating aspects of my practice through academic publication, it was at the start of my PhD that I started to view publishing as a key to my future career success. Subconsciously, I had therefore subscribed to the 'publish or perish' mantra, which has 'pervaded academia and increasingly taken its toll on academics' (Lee, 2014, p. 250). Surrounded by academics in a research-intensive university, it was hard not to see academic publishing, as Hangel and Schmidt-Pfister (2017) describe it, 'the *conditio sine qua non* across all career stages' (p. 533). Although I had not yet figured out how not to perish, I was convinced that my PhD would be the first step in that direction. I was thus ready to enter what De Rond and Miller (2005) call a 'race against time' as an aspiring academic seeking to succeed in a competitive industry.

My realisation that academic publishing would be the career-making step came with the growing awareness of hurdles to overcome. For a start, I had no publishing experience to draw upon. As a non-native English speaker, my language skills appeared to me as an issue – rightly or wrongly. Could I effectively communicate with scholars in the field? Though I am not alone in harbouring concerns about my abilities to write for publication during the PhD (see Merga, Mason, & Morris, 2019), my fears intensified very early on in my PhD journey as I discovered the status-signalling use of academic jargon (Brown, Anicich, & Galinsky, 2020). My moment came when, after a detailed presentation on my doctoral research, a fellow doctoral student asked: 'So, what is your *epistemology*?' because I had not used the word in the whole 20-minute talk. Thus, my desire to write for academic publication was as much an identity-affirming drive for peer acceptance and recognition as well as a career-building strategy (Hangel & Schmidt-Pfister, 2017) that required of me to embrace a new academic culture where I would become proficient in the language and jargon expected of those in this culture.

DEVELOPING AWARENESS OF PERSONAL SHORTCOMINGS: PLANNING FOR FAILURE

As implied above, I had absolutely no doubt that my initial attempt at getting my work published would not start off with roaring success. But I also didn't want this to come as a surprise. I wanted to plan my imminent rejections and learn as much as I could from the earlier ones before setting off with 'proper' writing from my PhD. It is from here that I started purposefully plotting how to celebrate the rejection of my papers! Far from being self-defeating, the steps taken (as detailed below) sought to minimise my perceived weaknesses to improve my future publication successes. Accordingly, I conceived a two-pronged plan. The first part of the plan was to bridge my skills gap through training. This was an easily achievable goal. Besides my university mandated research methods training, I took a range of research-focused trainings and workshops. In addition to my supervisors' mentorship. All this shaped my understanding of writing for an academic audience but did not give me hands-on writing experience. I would address this in the second part of the plan: practicing.

Having already identified journal editors and reviewers as the source of feedback (Merga et al., 2019), I knew that I needed to submit something worth their time, not some 'academic slime' – to borrow a term once used by a colleague to describe bad writing. How was I to practice career-making academic writing at low academic and emotional cost? By this, I mean finding a 'safe' academic writing environment where I could try publishing, fail and yet learn from the experience without worrying about rejections putting my doctoral work offtrack (Merga et al., 2019). My concerns were feeding off a workshop called *How to write a great research paper and get it accepted by a good journal* that I had attended in mid-2018. Led by a major academic publishing house, it opened with a slide called 'Why are you here?'. On the slide, a cartoonish depiction of an academic holding a paper they are taking through an unmistakably Darwinian walk towards the ultimate 'paper accepted' milestone.[1] The author-to-be had to walk through two rows of hostile beings wielding mace, sword, axe, the reaper's scythe and a gun, just in case! The characters are depicted in a 'ready-to-strike' position to the point that one could not help wondering, 'If academic publishing is like this, why bother?'

CONFUSION AND INDECISION: CONSIDERING THE PHD FORMAT

Between desire to do something and somewhat discouraging depictions of academic publishing journey, I was in a state of uncertainty, confusion and overall lack of strategy. A few days after that workshop, for example, I impulsively decided to change my PhD format from the 'traditional' route to a 'journal format' as a quick way to build up my publication portfolio (Merga et al., 2019). As I met my supervisors to

---

[1] https://blogger.googleusercontent.com/img/b/R29vZ2xl/AVvXsEjKbU0P2m
PjX0PfwEJEoca3fGEsVXqim4fyhogYQsT30Ww7o4AkfkKW2WBmGuiL7
9WsQoBgOuOF9UNRRf1S7Q3w7beo4dZ9r3IYrdgty1TKRFTghhjTcRFo
0TPOIpmxaFLyEDCBfdvPilMR/s1600/8.jpg

inform them of 'the decision', I started to see huge cracks in my argument. I was only concerned with getting more publications. I had not considered whether my research topic was best suited for the Journal Format, the impact of such a change at a later phase in my PhD and the other many limitations of the 'PhD by publication' route (Robins & Kanowski, 2008). After this episode, I decided to stick to my original PhD format and instead create an academic publishing playground where I could practise academic publication at low risk, keeping my PhD data for when I knew the craft of the academic publishing trade!

THE MOMENT OF RECKONING: BITTERSWEET REJECTIONS

As noted earlier, I had already been encouraged to write for publication and as part of this, I already had initiated work in this by collecting data on my practice though this went on hold at the start of the PhD. I had also started and then put on hold a plan to turn my MA dissertation into a journal paper. I saw these two projects as inconsequential works that I could submit to a journal, get rejected and still crack on with my PhD. In hindsight, it is easy to see that my goals were not mere pursuit of editors' constructive feedback but also an unconscious fear of the kind of emotional damage that a rejection of a paper based on my PhD would have on my motivation and confidence to hold onto the project. A major curiosity in the project was seeing if editors would think I had contributed to knowledge. Despite this being perceived as the 'ultimate criterion of value applied to academic research' (Elbanna & Child, 2023, p. 615), I was far from being able to boldly point at its contribution to knowledge. So, this was especially going to help me with the writing of my PhD research contribution.

Nevertheless, I finished one paper from my MA dissertation and another from my practitioner research I had done earlier and submitted both. For my effort to get constructive rejections, the journey started on a false note. The first rejection came back without the feedback I expected, only that the paper could not be published in their journal. I resubmitted the paper elsewhere, this time with more luck. Though still a desk rejection, the editor sent me useful feedback, explaining why it could not be published in their journal. I was happy with this feedback but rather unhappy with my embarrassing carelessness: some of the feedback included details I could have easily learnt from the journal aims, which I had only summarily read. Lesson learnt! Third time was the charm! I was able to respond to reviewers' feedback (for the first time), and the paper was accepted.

For my second paper, I used everything I learnt from the first two rejections. Going through the review process of the carefully selected journal was extremely instructional although (or maybe because) its review process was excruciatingly long to the point I had to be talked out of withdrawing the paper by a senior colleague. Reviewed by three anonymous reviewers in three rounds, this paper was an especially learning moment in dealing with reviewers' feedback. I had to reconcile sometimes contradictory comments from the reviewers and then respond to them justifying why I disagreed. Disagreeing with reviewers? This was an identity-shaping undertaking, especially with my own self-awareness as a not-yet-an-academic.

MOVING FORWARD, BUT WHERE?

In my search for constructive rejections, I discovered a lot about the academic publishing journey and myself as an aspiring academic. What I considered to be low-stake writing ended up on my CV (and not much from my PhD) when applying for jobs, though how this affected my employment chances remains unknown. Nevertheless, the perceived safety of this environment allowed me to build confidence and dare to engage with reviewers with a 'got nothing to lose' attitude. Looking back, it is hard to imagine the impact two consecutive rejections on a paper from my PhD would have had on my self-confidence and motivation as a research student. Although only one paper has now been published from my PhD and I have since embarked on other projects, practicing publishing on something other than my PhD work certainly allowed me to move forward as an aspiring academic without agonising in self-doubt.

Nevertheless, throughout the rejections and success, the experience taught me, more than anything else, that the 'process of producing quality academic research is challenging and meticulous' (Elbanna & Child, 2023, p. 614). I embarked on a journey to seek rejections on what I saw as less important projects undertaken before I was a PhD student. I was seeking these constructive rejections in the hope that this would shed more light on my academic writing and help me when I would be ready to finally write about my 'career-making work'. The need for this strategy emerged from a desire to succeed academically, using my PhD work as a starting point and the self-realisation of having no experience in academic paper publishing, as well as my worries about the new academic and linguistic cultures I was seeking to embrace. While this allowed me to get my earlier work published, it also meant that my doctoral work gathered dust when it shouldn't have.

The experience from my PhD led me to appreciate the value of engagement with editors and reviewers in the publication process; and the need to avoid the tunnel vision about getting published and career success. As Lee (2014, p. 251) observes 'even though academics do publish, they may still perish in the system if their publications do not meet the requirements laid down by their universities'. This is perhaps why sharing experiences like these might benefit those who are doing or planning to get started with academic publishing for all the right and wrong reasons imaginable.

REFERENCES

Brown, Z. C., Anicich, E. M., & Galinsky, A. D. (2020). Compensatory conspicuous communication: Low status increases jargon use. *Organizational Behavior and Human Decision Processes*, *161*, 274–290.

De Rond, M., & Miller, A. N. (2005). Publish or perish: Bane or boon of academic life? *Journal of Management Inquiry*, *14*(4), 321–329.

Elbanna, S., & Child, J. (2023). From 'publish or perish' to 'publish for purpose'. *European Management Review*, *20*(4), 614–618.

Hangel, N., & Schmidt-Pfister, D. (2017). Why do you publish? On the tensions between generating scientific knowledge and publication pressure. *Aslib Journal of Information Management*, *69*(5), 529–544.

Kwihangana, F. (2021). *Preservice language teachers' digital teacher identity development in an under-resourced context*. PhD Thesis. The University of Manchester.

Lee, I. (2014). Publish or perish: The myth and reality of academic publishing. *Language Teaching*, 47(2), 250–261.

Merga, M. K., Mason, S., & Morris, J. E. (2019). 'The constant rejections hurt': Skills and personal attributes needed to successfully complete a thesis by publication. *Learned Publishing*, 32(3), 271–281.

16

IT IS NOT EASY TO LEARN ABOUT YOUR ACADEMIC SELF THROUGH THE EYES OF REVIEWERS

MIRA BEKAR

Ss. Cyril and Methodius University, Republic of North Macedonia

As with Jess (Chapter 5), Mira is a more loosely associated member of the Lantern community – her connections arising from a joint project with Manchester colleagues rather than through doctoral study at Manchester. In fact, in this volume, hers is the only doctorate awarded outside the United Kingdom (Bekar, 2015). Since graduation, she has developed a portfolio of solo-authored (e.g., Bekar, 2022) and jointly authored (e.g., Bekar & Fay, 2020; Bekar & Yakhontova, 2021; Yakhontova & Bekar, 2024) work. Despite most of the authors in this volume having professional and academic 'homes' outside the English-speaking world, perhaps because of a strong English practitioner focus within Lantern, the issue of Anglo-based academic

(*Continued*)

> (*Continued*)
>
> norms is rarely mentioned. Mira's chapter is a noticeable exception. Her narrative is driven by a desire to understand why academia is positioned in the way it is and why the process of becoming a member of the Anglo-based academic community is not smooth even after studying in a US university. The key concept emerging from her chapter is that of academic 'self.' Among other conclusions she reaches is that blind reviews can often be unproductive.

INTRODUCTION AND MOTIVATION

Since 2005, I have been involved in learning about, practising and teaching academic writing in English as L2. Among other responsibilities I have instructed students how to write academic papers, pass writing exams on standardised tests, write theses and publish research articles. In 2005, I initiated a University Writing Project in collaboration with the British Council with the aim of developing a four-year syllabus for academic writing courses at the English Department where I work. Until 2006, my exposure to academic writing was largely Macedonian-based with few Anglo-oriented experiences, but during my Fulbright visit in the United States and my enrolment as a PhD student at a US university, I was exposed fully to an Anglo-centred understanding of academic literacy. For my Master's studies and then for my PhD thesis (Bekar, 2015), written in the area of Applied Linguistics, in the Second Language Studies Programme, I got fully engaged in what it means to be successful as an academic writer in the

Anglo-centred world. In my case, the journey so far is more about trying to understand why academia is positioned in the way it is and why the process of becoming a member of the Anglo-based academic community is not smooth even after obtaining your education abroad; it is actually a struggle in which one keeps on reflecting on the academic 'self.'

My professional passion revolved around qualitative studies on shared communicative and writing experiences. This means that naturally I love being engaged in recollection, reflection and social interaction – the emotional investment in academia. Then, there is this interest of mine in the 'self' and its construction in the postmodern market society and the whole idea about the enactment of ethical and ideological commitments as well as my existence in the world of a Macedonian-based versus English-based academic context.

In this narrative, my experiences with publishing co-authored work as a young scholar a few years after obtaining my PhD are presented. The aim is to analyse the creation of my academic *self* through the comments of the reviewers and the strategies I negotiated with my co-authors to 'satisfy' the reviewers. In order to achieve my aim, I drew on Labov's narrative analysis (1972, 1997, 2006). The narrative focuses on the reviewers' comments, the feelings and the strategies negotiated between my co-authors and my academic *self* to 'win or quit the battle' with the reviewers and editors for two particular book chapters for edited collections.

THEORETICAL UNDERPINNINGS BUZZING IN MY HEAD

As a linguist, I have been exposed to the narrative analysis scheme suggested by Labov, who defined narrative 'as a particular way of reporting past events, in which the order of a sequence of independent clauses is interpreted as the order of the events referred to' (Labov, 2006, p. 37). His framework helps to reveal the structure of the narrative by deconstructing it into constitutive and consecutive elements, which he appropriately labelled as follows: Abstract (Introduces the story to be told), Orientation (presents preliminary information on participants, space and time settings, and relevant previous actions), Complicating action (disrupts the usual chain of events leading to a crisis), Evaluation (creates a feeling of suspense by providing evaluation of narrative events), Resolution (shows how the crisis is resolved), and Coda (produces a sense of completion by bringing a reader back to the starting point of a story). So, I came up with an idea of classifying the reviewers' comments and the decisions I have made with my co-authors into Labov's categories focusing on complicating action, evaluation and resolution. Narrate in order to reflect.

THE ACTUAL EVENTS

After having collected the comments from four reviewers on two papers, I did a linguistic analysis trying to understand, in an analytical and reflective way, what it is in the nature of comments that brings frustration and mental block at times and slows down the revision process. I am happy to say that content comments prevailed over the language ones. I also believe that reviewers are not aware of how the major three elements of the Labov's complicating action, evaluation and resolution play complex roles.

Let us look at two examples of reviewers' comments which portray the 'complicating action,' basically answering the question 'What has disrupted the usual chain of events that led to a crisis?'

Example 1

In one case, the reviewer commented on our results. He wrote:

The statement of results [...] that the interviews show a certain narrative structure is vacuous since they assumed and looked for it (ref above re deductive or inductive structure; changing the structure wouldn't change the process of the study of course but might be more convincing to readers).

For two L2 speakers of English whose first languages are non-English related, this comment just made us think how the language used in peer reviews (e.g., 'vacuous') can be perceived as overly critical and distressing, especially by new coming L2 researchers. The first meaning of 'vacuous' that comes to mind is 'empty' and 'mindless'. I wondered who was 'mindless': us, as authors, not carefully considering our academic writing or the interviewees' input? What does the 'process of the study' refer to and how would referencing a 'deductive or inductive structure' make the paper more convincing? This confusion stems not just from language choice but also from our lack of familiarity as new, non-Anglo-based researchers with all the communicative purposes and linguistic nuances of academic writing genres. Our point was that transcribed interviews, as hybrids of oral interaction and written coherent narrative, can be analysed for their textual structures and discursive practices. However, we did not sound convincing with the idea that a structural framework of universal organisational patterns assumes that context produces certain discourses which construct the interviewees' version of reality; however, we were accused of assuming that a certain narrative structure existed in the interviews and then specifically looked for evidence of it. This meant for us that the outcome was predetermined in the eyes of the reviewer.

Example 2

Example 2 is a portrayal of intellectual commenting that leads nowhere and is non-efficient for the authors. My claim was that:

> *Christiansen (2020) basing her work on Benor (2010) explains that the ethnolinguistic repertoire is a dynamic set of linguistic resources available to individuals within an ethnic group, used variably to express their ethnic identities and that this concept allows for a nuanced analysis of linguistic variation, accounting for diverse social dimensions within a community.*

The reviewer's comment stated: 'The concept in itself doesn't allow for anything; it is only when you analyse your data from the point of view of a concept like that it begins to allow for anything.'

This is one of the moments when you feel like quitting academia, without turning back, because of this 'academic' discourse called 'the concept of the concept about the concept' and the mentality of the traditionally perceived notion of what academia should look like: being an important scholar is about being occluded. If I had had the chance to ask the reviewer what he/she had meant, I would have tried to clarify whether the problem is in the difference between a concept as an abstract idea and its practical application in my analysis or is it about guiding the reader through my interpretation of the data, allowing the readers to derive meaning or conclusions from it. And, in the end, it seems that we might be talking about the same thing, i.e., that a concept becomes meaningful when it is used as a lens through which data is analysed. Who knows.

The above comments are representative examples of 'complicating action' comments which, unfortunately, authors can't efficiently implement in their revisions.

EVALUATION AND RESOLUTION

According to Labov, the 'evaluation' produces the effect of tension and suspense. It provides information on the consequences of the complication for the feelings, needs and desires of an individual – it answers the question 'So what?' This question is what I have asked myself or my co-authors many times when receiving reviewers' comments. The evaluation can be traced in the two examples below.

Example 3

Our paper was about happy end stories of thesis writers. We clearly stated the purpose about happy ends, meaning 'the successful completion and defence of a thesis – as a kind of victory, and the student himself or herself – as a winner in the struggle with difficult situations and circumstances.' However, the reviewer complication occurred when he/she emphasised:

> *They [i.e., the authors] also claim that the happy-end stories are explained by the retrospective and forget one of the more serious limitations of the collection*

> *of only having successful students in it...what would have happened if non-completers were interviewed, or those whose texts were not accepted?*

But dear reviewer, we did not want to interview the non-completers since the aim was to interview writers who completed the whole journey of the thesis writing and to explore success and happiness! Why should someone always play the devil advocate's role?

My critical action here would be to emphasise the necessity to further examine how the words of negative and positive evaluation interact in the anonymous peer review process and understand its evaluative function. With my co-author, we agreed that it's important to note that evaluative words in peer reviews carry significant illocutionary force, especially since the genre requires explicit critical assessment. These evaluative terms can strongly impact how authors perceive the feedback on their papers emotionally. We/the authors resolved this issue by posing a question/adding a recommendation about future research on finding out whether similar patterns would be identified among students who failed their theses.

Example 4

With my students, I refer to the next type of comments as 'Praise first and then knock 'em down' approach. And it is always Reviewer 2 who is worse, they say. In our case Reviewer 2 seemed like an angel but after praising our work by saying 'This is one of the chapters I looked forward to reading and is one, among many, of the reasons this volume stands out for me as an original and much needed contribution to the literature. The knocking down occurred in the 'I want to see more' approach. One of the biggest frustrations of authors is word limit, the complexity of a topic to be packed in small packages. The question that troubles writers is why reviewers rarely suggest ways of cutting out some material but love to say 'I would like to see more discussion here or a reference to other chapters that will take up your questions,' 'there probably should be some discussion' or 'unpack it.'

Resolution? As authors, we just added a reference to one of the other chapters in the collection, a step that was encouraged by the editors.

Similar to this are the instances of the highest extreme a reviewer can present – the approach of 'The paper is not good but I am here to help.' The exact comment I received in the past was, 'You will not like my comments; you will not want to re-write as much as I suggest. All the same, let's see what you make of it and then we can talk,' adding 'my editorial reading is strategic and I'm trying to make your paper more convincing.'

In this instance, the reviewer extrapolates their own professional knowledge and experience to encompass that of other researchers, urging the recipients, as highlighted by de Hoop and Hogeweg (2014, p. 4), to empathise and see from another perspective. However, in the above passage, this suggestion takes on a negative connotation since it sounds as if the reviewer implicitly criticises the author as less competent.

The situations of vivid emotional tension naturally lead to the 'resolution' stage and the overcoming of the crisis. The sudden impetus that occurs in us/authors to overcome the surrounding problems and successfully reach the stage of a paper acceptance is a clear example of how intentionality of individuals wins the battle in the academic ecological system.

REFLECTION: WHAT I HAVE LEARNT

As a young scholar, I've learnt that collaborative work is more fruitful than individual authorship if you find the collaborators that make your work challenging and inspirational. The reviewers' comments can be harsh, so having the chance for a dialogue with a co-author sharing the burden of decisions what to do in the revision process is valuable for the self-confidence, self-worth as an academic and mental encouragements to respond properly to the reviewers or editors' requirements. Dialogues in which co-authors discuss reviewers' comments that are unclear are not rare. As one of my co-authors said recently, 'I will accumulate all my patience and will try to add some explanations. Will this difficult story ever end? 😢'. Truly, if the comments are just about intellectualising concepts rather than revision-related comments offering concrete steps for improvements, that suggests a need for further academic discussion/dialogue that should be done at a conference or individually.

Establishing emotional credibility should be built: An important lesson. The presence of such a strategy requires that the audience believe in the truthfulness, occurrence and form of the events described in the story, just as Labov (1997) explains it. Emotionally sharing our experience of handling reviewers' comments is an important step. Emotional credibility goes with honest admitting about unclear power roles and 'blind' communication. The possible miscommunication between publishing houses, editors, and individuals who are required to write responses to chapters for free with all the power games and work overload included, always seems to crash on the authors' heads because, ultimately, they are the ones who need to juggle in the long 'blind' reviewing processes. The communicative situation which gives rise to the genre of an anonymous review is that of 'teacher and pupil'

(Burrough-Boenisch, 2003), which often is perceived as didactic pathos instead of professional guidance and a helpful insight.

One of my co-authors observed that three factors play significant roles in the reviewing process: safeguarding academic standards from unsuitable papers, the reviewer's status as an expert, and anonymity, which shapes how both authors and reviewers represent themselves. I would add that blind reviews can be unproductive, as unclear comments tend to overshadow the need for clarity and reasonableness. This leads authors to focus more on appeasing reviewers and on 'finding a way out' in order to thrive in academia.

REFERENCES

Bekar, M. (2015). *Language, writing, and social (inter) action: An analysis of text-based chats in Macedonian and English*. PhD dissertation. Purdue University.

Bekar, M. (2022). Interculturality and interdisciplinarity in bachelor thesis writing: Mentors' and mentees' perceptions. *Journal of Contemporary Philology*, 5(2), 77–91.

Bekar, M., & Fay, R. (2020). Developing Anglo-centred academic literacy: Problematizing understandings of criticality. In A. Simpson & F. Dervin (Eds.), *The meaning of criticality in education research: Reflecting on critical pedagogy* (pp. 23–45). Palgrave Macmillan.

Bekar, M., & Yakhontova, T. (2021). Dimensions of student writer's *self* in qualitative research interviews. In L.-M. Muresan & C. Orna-Montesinos (Eds.), *Academic literacy development: Perspectives on multilingual scholars' approaches to writing* (pp. 185–206). Springer.

Benor, S. B. (2010). Ethnolinguistic repertoire: Shifting the analytic focus in language and ethnicity. *Journal of Sociolinguistics*, *14*, 159–183. https://doi.org/10.1111/j.1467-9841.2010.00440.x

Burrough-Boenisch, J. (2003). Shapers of published NNS research articles. *Journal of Second Language Writing*, *12*(3), 223–243.

Christiansen, M. S. (2020). Identity and empowerment: Vernacular English features used by bilingual Mexicans online. *Language@Internet*, *18*. https://scholarworks.iu.edu/journals/index.php/li/article/view/37789

de Hoop, H., & Hogeweg, L. (2014). The use of second person pronouns in a literary work. *Journal of Literary Semantics*, *43*(2), 109–125. https://doi.org/10.1515/jls-2014-0008

Labov, W. (1972). *Language in the inner city: Studies in the Black English vernacular*. University of Pennsylvania Press.

Labov, W. (1997). Some further steps in narrative analysis. *Journal of Narrative & Life History*, *7*(1–4), 395–415.

Labov, W. (2006). Narrative pre-construction. *Narrative Inquiry*, *16*(1), 37–45.

Yakhontova, T., & Bekar, M. (2024). How thesis writers speak about their experiences: A linguistic perspective. In B. Petrić & M. Castelló (Eds.), *Students' bachelor's and master's thesis writing journeys: A transnational European perspective*. Multilingual Matters.

17

IT'S NOT ABOUT ME

PAUL VINCENT SMITH

The University of Manchester, UK

Paul is currently a Lecturer in Education at The University of Manchester where he completed his doctoral studies (Smith, 2013). Since graduation, he has published two solo-authored works (Smith, 2021, 2022) from, or related to, his thesis and is developing a portfolio of mainly co-authored works (e.g., Baratta & Smith, 2019; Smith & Baratta, 2016) arising from other projects. His narrative concerns an infrequently discussed area of publishing – controversial topics and the reviewer's controversial positioning of the author's intentionalities. He, like many of the other contributors to this volume, sees advantages in co-authorship, not least the better authorial decision-making that collaborative work may force on authors.

INTRODUCTION

As one of my erstwhile doctoral supervisors is fond of saying, *everything gets published eventually*. I find this to be a typically loaded comment. It says something *about* a lot of things: the academic publishing industry; the variable quality of academic publication taken as an ever-increasing body of work and the nature of knowledge itself. It also says something *to* the individual writer-researcher. What can be read superficially as a slogan of encouragement can rapidly become a cause for reflection. If we envisage, or are compelled into publishing only 'eventually,' is it worth publishing at all? Is this the right form in which to attempt publication? Where rejection has been experienced, which of my choices have been instrumental in this? I find that part of researcher expertise is developing a sense of when to cut one's losses, and when to persevere. This chapter is in part a story of perseverance. Most of all, though, it concerns questions of attribution made of the author by reviewers themselves trying to make sense of what they see. These questions have culminated in an extended reflective self-critique.

WRITING ABOUT CONTROVERSIAL DATA

One of the most generative experiences of my PhD studies, one that has taken on almost a life of its own, was finding a few short passages in a transcript from an interview with a rather unforthcoming second-year undergraduate. These passages constituted a narrative sufficient to sustain an extended analytical case study. I have found over the years that the gist of this case is easily communicable in lay terms, so here goes: There is a student who describes herself as a born-again Christian. She studies social sciences. In her second year, she takes a course in sociological theories of gender and sexuality.[1] She has to write an essay on a quote asserting that, when it comes to gender and sexuality, 'nature has nothing to do with it.' Openly uneasy with this premise, she needs to find ways of (a) producing a piece of recognisable undergraduate sociology while (b) writing nothing that openly contradicts her beliefs. Describing her practical and textual methods for achieving these dual aims formed the analytic purpose of my chapter.

Later, in my immediate post-doctoral era, I attempted to write up this case in publishable form. This proved to be more difficult than I had anticipated. Despite dedicating the necessary care to selecting potential journals, many rejected the paper. In one case, the rejection took a mere morning and in another case, several months and two rounds of extensive corrections. The latter rejection did at least make me realise that the paper was in far superior form at the end of the amendment process than it had been at the beginning. So certainly, at first, quality was part of the reason for this piece hanging around in publication purgatory. In other cases, the following reasons were cited for rejection: lack of relevance to the journal's aims; analysis too broad (or too narrow) and too much data (or data that were not rich enough). Sometimes, I was told that I needed to make a choice between writing an empirical or a policy article.

In the meantime, the ideas in this unpublished piece had, ironically, developed into a whole research agenda. Word of my work had spread to a now-close colleague, who asked if I had anything that might be turned into a larger project. I said that I had a case study of a student of faith; it was a single

---

[1] If you've stopped reading to consult this footnote, I suggest that this case is already readable as one where some 'trouble' may occur. We can readily infer some of the behaviours and values, even if in broad terms, that might accompany the identity of 'born-again Christian.'

example, but there was a nascent literature behind it, and it seemed plausible that other examples (of the potential 'conflict' between religion and academic demands) could readily be revealed. In this view, I was encouraged by attending a Society for Research into Higher Education seminar in London just after my graduation, in which the presenters and delegates themselves outlined related examples. So it happened that we won both external and internal research funding and produced corresponding publications (Baratta & Smith, 2019; Smith & Baratta, 2016), before the material that inspired this research ever saw the light of day. However, I still thought of the original case as paradigmatic, not least for the availability of detailed and contemporary data materials available therein. This, then, was a publication to persevere with.

ENGAGING WITH REVIEWER FEEDBACK

There were two comments on submitted drafts that took my attention. The comments were from different journals and make more or less identical inferences about me *qua* the author although from completely polarised perspectives. Both referred to me as 'partisan' in this term or in near synonyms. However, where one saw me as critiquing the student on the basis of her conservative Christianity, the other review understood my work as promulgating her attitudes, colluding in a 'dangerous' offensive on social constructivism.

Needless to say, I saw myself very much as doing neither. My concern was to provide a *descriptive* analysis of the visible practices in both text and talk that the case study yielded. The categories, narrative, and materials I used were the student's own, and my aim was to anchor my procedure and conclusions concretely in what she had said and written. Other analyses are possible, and I provided enough information to allow for alternatives. Further, I saw no contradiction in conducting a descriptive analysis while also suggesting that the outcomes of the analysis would contribute to a body of work of interest to university-based scholars and leaders. This all seemed, simply, interesting in itself. What appeared to me a set of defensible claims put forward on that basis nonetheless led me to be buffeted against the barriers of the straight-and-narrow strictures of journal scope.

I find that there are two possibilities for reflection at this point. One is to think about how reviewers approach this kind of material. The reviewers and editors did (and generally do) a systematic job with full reference to journal aims. Replicating, in a minor way, the reconstructive method of the article itself (now published as Smith, 2022), I found myself wanting to find the methods for arriving at the reviewer comments (rather than, say, empathising with or complaining about the reviewers). A second possibility is to think about this as a learning experience for the academic writer wishing to be published. Here, I focus on this latter possibility.

The struggle within the narrative above occasioned a great deal of thought about the subjectivity of the reviewer who acts on behalf of a journal; and the subjectivity of the author who is writing among other things for the approval of the reviewer. It is clear to me that these struggles have occurred less frequently, and their emotional and practical effects have been much diluted, by writing in a pair or a team. Whether this is necessarily so is itself a useful locus for reflection; but in any case, the joint-authored pieces that are referenced here did not go through anything like this route to publication. Those were, relatively, very smooth experiences.

THE EFFECT OF CO-AUTHORSHIP

Some of the above is perhaps attributable to journal choice, but it is not as though I did not spend copious amounts of time selecting journal titles for the piece whose history I outline here. It could be that the moderating effect of co-authorship, and the additional discipline that this forces on writers, contributes to better decisions. If the writing partnership, or team, is working to its best effect, then the submission needs to meet the aims and requirements of multiple authors before it ever reaches a reviewer's desk. Learning and exercising the art of compromise in a friendly setting, where joint authors will generally quickly arrive at a common agenda, is a useful scaffold in approaching journals where the unwritten rules of engagement are often not knowable in advance. If one thinks about being published as a chain of events that all need to happen for the publication to happen, I find also that writing collaboratively provides a series of shortcuts along the way; the number and magnitude of choices and decisions just seems to be that much easier.

It's certainly not the case that collaborative writing will always dissuade reviewers from concluding that the authors are on some kind of crusade. I have seen reviewer comments – on writers other than myself, to be clear – that bluntly conclude in this way. However, joint authorship attenuates the extent to which such comments can be 'personal.' Rather than being about me (or not), it's about us. ('Perhaps the reviewer was thinking of the bit I didn't write?')

A final insight that occurs to me is that in my many failed attempts to publish my original article, I essentially gave the reviewers a lot of work to do: follow conceptual arguments; work through data, and connect to current debates not only in academia but also in higher education equalities. One could argue that reviewers should be able to handle many threads;

but in finally selecting a journal that has a specific interest in social science methodology, they were able to use a single lens to apprehend my work – and at last, it seemed to make sense for someone else. I have, I think, refined a sense of what can and should be attempted, both by me as the author and by those who will collaborate on publication.

REFERENCES

Baratta, A., & Smith, P. V. (2019). The confrontation of identities: How university students manage academic and religious selves in higher education. *Educational Studies*, *45*(6), 771–786. https://doi.org/10.1080/03055698.2018.1534084

Smith, P. V. (2013). *Academic literacy practices: Plausibility in the essays of a diverse social science cohort*. PhD Thesis. The University of Manchester.

Smith, P. V. (2021). Abduction in the academy: The mysteries of academic writing as a pragmatic problem for students in higher education. *Ethnographic Studies*, *18*, 75–98.

Smith, P. V. (2022). 'In universities, the religious people keep their mouths shut': Solving an interdiscursive problem in higher education literacy practices. *Forum Qualitative Sozialforschung Forum: Qualitative Social Research*, *23*(3). https://doi.org/10.17169/fqs-23.3.3891

Smith, P. V., & Baratta, A. (2016). Religion and literacies in higher education: Scoping the possibilities for faith-based meaning making. *Critical Studies in Teaching and Learning (CriSTaL)*, *4*(2), 68–87.

COMMENTARY TO PART E

RICHARD FAY[a] AND ACHILLEAS KOSTOULAS[b]

[a]The University of Manchester, UK
[b]University of Thessaly, Greece

Part E is, in some ways, different from the parts of the book that preceded it. The narratives in this part of the book all focus on the final stages of publication and engagement with the peer-review and publication processes. Inevitably, such a discussion brings to the fore issues of differences in perspective, epistemic justice and power. They also suggest how these issues may be constructively resolved by complementing and affirming the authors' identities.

A common theme in some of these narratives is that they illustrate what Stelma and Kostoulas (2021, 2024) describe as 'purposive' activity in an ecology. Unlike normative and creative activity, purposive activity in academic writing involves deliberately creating opportunities for action that are consistent with one's desired trajectory and then acting on them. Duygu's series of vignettes, which illustrate dilemmas and challenges associated with publishing collectively, tell the story of how an early career researcher can purposively navigate their academic ecology in order to achieve her desired goals. Similarly, Felix's deliberate strategy of using the structure of the publication system to create opportunities for him to develop illustrates the kind of confident academic becoming that is expected as a doctoral student or an ECR matures academically. In Part A, academic becoming was defined as a process of moving towards a space of full participation in an ecology – these two narratives point towards what such a space might look like.

A second commonality in some narratives is the dialogic understanding of the writing process. Our use of the word 'dialogic' here is based loosely on the Bakhtinian proposal that one understands oneself through the perspective of others (Bakhtin, 1981/1975).

Mira Bekar's series of interactions with reviewers highlight the challenges of engaging with ones writing as reflected back by other readers, especially when this re-reading is complicated by power differentials. In a similar way, Paul Smith's narrative shows the complications involved in reading a text that was produced by a study participant, re-told by him in his authorial capacity and reflected back to him by the reviewers.

If one tried to condense ecological theory to a single phrase, that would be 'it's all connected.' Mira and Paul's contributions show us ways to betted understand these interconnections, as we re-encounter our work seen through the perspective of others. Duygu and Felix show how awareness of the ecology's structure can be used to achieve desired outcomes. Collectively, these four chapters remind us that, if everything shapes everything else, these dense feedback looks can be used to drive publication efforts.

REFERENCES

Bakhtin, M. M. (1981). *The dialogic imagination: Four essays* (M. Holquist, ed., C. Emmerson & M. Holquist, trans.). University of Texas Press. (Original work published in Russian in 1975).

Stelma, J., & Kostoulas, A. (2021). *The intentional dynamics of TESOL*. De Gruyter Mouton.

Stelma, J., & Kostoulas, A. (2024). Revisiting complex dynamic systems theory: Empowering language teachers and teaching. *TESOL Journal, 15*(3), e790.

18

CONCLUDING COMMENTS

MIRA BEKAR

Ss. Cyril and Methodius University, Republic of North Macedonia

The journey through 15 narratives by authors from 11 countries approached its end. The/our chapters covered a variety of topics related to academic writing and publishing, as well as professional growth within the academic field. The idea that plays a key role in all chapters is the idea of 'intentionality,' referring to the understanding of how individuals purposefully use their writing and literacy abilities. 'Intentionality' may be approached as a 'purpose for action' or as existence (and survival) in a certain context. When individuals or groups act with a specific purpose guiding their behaviour, they are said 'to act intentionally.' This understanding has been presented in philosophical and cognitive approaches to science. In the past (Bekar & Fay, 2020), we have problematised the concept of 'criticality' and critical thinking skills in the process of developing Anglo-centred academic literacy using the ecological perception of critical intentional action as defined by Fay and Stelma (2016) and Stelma and Fay (2019). All the contributors in this book constantly wonder using the critical lens what our students and we ourselves are handling in order to thrive in different academic contexts, i.e. that we all have intentions and have to find ways to realise them.

The ecology of our existence is a complex mix of the ecology of intention, the existence in parallel usually linguistic contexts, the maturation of our understanding how to recognise and use the affordances around us and the development of our skills for critical action.

The contexts in which all book contributors exist are often categorised as Anglophone and non-Anglophone at the national level, but some of their doctoral programs were delivered in English within institutions in countries where English is not an official language.

Questions such as *Who am I? Who am I as….? Where are you from? What is your paper's unique selling point?* embody a complex intersection of linguistic, academic and even racial identities, which often influences one's self-perception and academic journey. During doctoral thesis writing, candidates inevitably face the challenge of completing their work and moving forward in the ecological system. The evolution in that system is evident in the truthfulness of the narratives. From 'waned interest,' 'anxious seeking of topic,' 'a second-class academic,' 'not equal to colleagues and their intellectuality,' 'increasingly vulnerable,' 'atypical writing,' 'more pressure,' 'impostor syndrome,' 'getting lost,' 'darkness,' 'become demoralised,' 'intensified fears' and 'frequent struggles', the contributors move towards creation of supportive systems, brightness, clear navigation, mindfulness, epistemic justice, intercultural ethics, researcher independence and emotional credibility.

Each ecological system sets the need for survival strategies. The exact strategies contributors mention relate to seeking collaborative opportunities with other researchers, publishing on diverse topics, academic growth, collaboration with co-authors, and navigating the publishing landscape. The courage to chart a specific path for one's research career has been a crucial aspect of everybody's academic journey. This internal struggle pushed us to reevaluate how we valued our academic worth, leading us to recognise and embrace our contributions beyond mere publication metrics. All of us use our own research on identity to validate and acknowledge the lived experiences of individuals, understanding the 'imagined community.' Contributors often questioned whether a clear purpose in research is always evident from the start or if it emerges gradually through the process. We learnt that the execution of the research projects can deviate from initial plans. We discovered the value of engaging with the academic community through platforms like ResearchGate or LinkedIn, which increase the visibility and impact of our research but also fostered a sense of belonging and professional identity. Moreover, working within a positive, non-judgemental and collaborative environment provides a much-needed respite. Being part of a supportive team allow us to regain confidence and alleviate the negative feelings.

Throughout these journeys presented through valuable theoretical frameworks of respected scholars and thinkers, we want to emphasise that human development does not cease upon moving to a new environment; rather, it is through intense intercultural and professional interactions that the individual is shaped in profound ways. Another learnt strategy is conceiving plans focused on targeted training and practice to produce work, which is worth the scholarly community's attention, but also finding a 'safe' academic writing environment where we could engage with constructive criticism without the fear of harsh judgement. However, the journeys of the book contributors also highlighted the compromises that researchers often feel compelled to make. In their efforts to succeed in academia, some become more focused on satisfying reviewers' expectations and finding ways to get their work accepted, sometimes at the expense of originality or quality.

This tension reflects the broader struggle within academic publishing, where both authors and reviewers bring their biases and perspectives to the process. It raises important questions about how much of what gets published truly advances knowledge versus merely conforms to the subjective standards of reviewers. As scholars committed to developing 'criticality,' we must navigate these complexities thoughtfully, striving for a balance between meeting the expectations of the field and maintaining the integrity and innovation of our research.

Multilingual skills have a profound effect on cognitive functions, enhancing abilities such as empathy and cultural awareness, which are crucial for navigating varied social and professional settings. This influence fosters insights that emerge through reflection. As the authors of the chapters in this book, we view ourselves as reflective individuals. Our reflective processes frequently involve using different languages based on the context or subject matter, demonstrating our adaptability to diverse environments. This is evident in our openness to unique concepts associated with specific languages, our awareness of when to adjust our language or integrate key terms from various languages to achieve mutual understanding.

We hope this book will inspire you to think about academia as a unique ecological system, to think how we thrive in varying social and professional contexts and how we may use language, writing and reflection as social action. Sharing experiences like ours could be valuable for those who are beginning their journey in the doctoral studies or academic publishing, whether for the right or wrong reasons, as it highlights the importance of perseverance and strategic planning in navigating this challenging process.

REFERENCES

Bekar, M., & Fay, R. (2020). Developing Anglo-centric literacy: Problematizing understandings of criticality. In A. Simpson & F. Dervin (Eds.), *The meanings of criticality in education research: Reflecting on critical pedagogy* (pp. 23–45). Palgrave Macmillan.

Fay, R., & Stelma, J. (2016). Criticality, intentionality and intercultural action. In M. Dasli & A. R. Díaz (Eds.), *The critical turn in language and intercultural communication pedagogy* (pp. 150–164). Routledge.

Stelma, J., & Fay, R. (2019). An ecological perspective for critical action in applied linguistics. In A. Kostoulas (Ed.), *Challenging boundaries in language education* (pp. 51–69). Springer.

www.ingramcontent.com/pod-product-compliance
Lightning Source LLC
Chambersburg PA
CBHW071740150426
43191CB00010B/1647